MIMESIS
INTERNATIONAL

AESTHETICS
n. 8

Pietro Conte

UNFRAMING AESTHETICS

www.mimesisinternational.com
e-mail: info@mimesisinternational.com

Book series: *Aesthetics*, n. 8

Isbn: 9788869772221

P.I. C.F. 02419370305

Cover image: John Chervinsky, *Bananas in Bowl with Painting on Table*, 2010, Walker Art Center, Minneapolis. Courtesy Kirsten Chervinsky

TABLE OF CONTENTS

To Maia,
who started teaching me
what it means to hold on
when she was still learning
to pull herself up to stand.

ACKNOWLEDGEMENTS

This book benefited from funding from the Portuguese Foundation for Science and Technology through the 'Investigator' programme. That it was ever completed owes much to Andrea Pinotti and all the members of the an-iconology team. I am indebted to Elio Franzini for granting me the opportunity to discuss some crucial aspects of the aesthetics of framing and unframing during a series of seminars held at the State University of Milan. My deepest gratitude goes to my parents for their constant encouragement and the many insightful suggestions throughout the writing process; to Daniele Molinini for his daily support during the Lisbon years and beyond; to Sarah De Sanctis, Michael FitzGerald, and Federica Cavaletti for assisting me in preparing the final manuscript; and to Doralice, who once promised to be always by my side, and this is exactly where she has been ever since.

INTRODUCTION

As a lovely frame adds to a painting,
Even though it is from a master's brush,
An indefinable strangeness and charm
By isolating it from vast nature...

Charles Baudelaire, *A Phantom*

We live surrounded by frames. Door frames, window frames; painting, photography, poster, billboard frames; television and cinema screen frames; desktop, laptop, tablet, mobile phone frames. Frames are so ubiquitous that we barely notice them. And yet, although we are all most familiar with every kind of framing devices, as soon as we try to characterise them more precisely, we find ourselves in a quandary. In philosophy, and more specifically in aesthetics, many attempts have been made to answer the Socratic *ti esti* question by providing an exhaustive, all-embracing description of the "true essence" of frames. However, they have often led not only to many contradictory definitions, but also, even worse, to normative claims about what a "good" frame should or ought to look like.

Instead of trying to detail what frames *are*, this book focuses on what they *do*. Its purpose is not to sketch out an ontology or a morphology of "the" frame, since it concentrates on frames *qua* agents, not *qua* objects. The assumption is that frames possess agency, meaning that they have a peculiar, frame-specific impact upon the beholder. Thus, the emphasis is on the processes and procedures of framing rather than on frames as concrete objects.

What does the act of framing amount to? What are its salient features? And how to distinguish it from other seemingly analogous operations? These questions are addressed in the first chapter, which starts from the almost self-evident truth that to consider something worth framing means to regard it as worth protecting and treasuring because of its unique affective power. To frame something is to draw attention to its specialness and to establish a clear-cut demarcation line between the usual and the unusual, the ordinary and the extraordinary. By separating a given object from its surroundings, the gesture of framing isolates it and makes it iconic, in the etymological sense of the word: it turns it into an *eikon*, it makes it an image.

This "iconising" quality is what directly and inextricably links frames to aesthetics, meant as both the science of art and the theory of perception. Traditionally, scholars have focused on the role of frames in relation to artworks, and especially to paintings. No wonder then that, when thinking of frames, the first things that come to mind are *picture* frames. To frame is to symbolise the work of art as a self-contained and self-sufficient aesthetic whole, thus strengthening the double function of its boundaries: exercising indifference towards (and defence against) the exterior while at the same time unifying the interior.

However, this also applies, far more broadly, to visual objects that are *not* works of art. Indeed, frames can even remain empty, circumscribing nothing but a void. In this case, they seem capable of turning whatever happens to enter their space – no matter what it is – into an image. To be more precise: they invite viewers to look at the framed object as something of major symbolic importance that not only requires special attention but also demands to be apprehended in a particular manner, namely, through a specific mode of consciousness.

This is crucial to understanding the power of framing. Aesthetically, frames do not merely define the reality (or rather, as we shall see, the quasi-reality) status of the visual objects enclosed within them as distinguished from the ordinary objects of daily life. They also ask viewers to consider the framed object not as a part of the world in which they live and act, but as a statement about that world – as a *representation* carrying symbolic meaning. From both a physical and a phenomenological point of view, frames act as gaze-directing devices: on the one hand, they "catch the eye" of the beholder and call attention to the enclosed objects; on the other hand, they demand a proper *modalisation* of the gaze. By marking a threshold between actual reality and the "unreality" of representation, the frame serves as a border at which our gaze is adjusted, reorganised, and reprogrammed. It causes estrangement, acting as a disorientation zone; but at the same time it provides a *new* orientation in that it instructs the observer on how to look at the framed object in order to apprehend it properly. This means that, while isolating the object from all that surrounds it and, therefore, from the viewer as well, the frame also helps this very same viewer to adopt the attitude necessary to *aesthetically* enjoy the framed object.

In this sense, the margins of representation are the borders of pleasurable mimesis, aesthetic illusion, and pretence. All framing devices have the effect of sharply demarcating the boundaries of the representational space by ensuring both the island-like structure of pictures and the beholder's awareness of being in front of "nothing but images". This also holds true for the particular subset of framing devices that includes so-called "institutional" frames. Museums and art galleries, for instance, do not only physically delimit a space purposely designed for exhibiting certain kinds of objects; they also define a field of orientation and expectation, in the sense that visitors must comply with specific rules and requirements in order to be able to appreciate the framed objects not as part of the visual continuum of everyday life but as salient types of artefacts. Therefore, even if there is certainly truth in the saying that the nature of all cultural objects depends on the context in which they are being considered, one should also never forget that context means framework: it results from – literally – the work of the frame, that is, from a gesture of framing.

The very presence of the frame invites the observer to switch from the spatio-temporal coordinates of actual reality to the fictional, knowingly illusory, "as-if" coordinates of representation. To put it into phenomenological terms: perception must give way to a quasi-perceptual state of image consciousness. Contrary to actual reality, the world of representation is defined by three basic properties: *mediateness*, *referentiality*, and *separateness*. All of these qualities are necessary for something to be called a representation of something else: if even one of them is missing, then there can be neither representation nor image consciousness.

By ensuring separateness, the frame has long been considered an integral part of the *dispositif* of representation, that is, a mechanism that every representation must include – to quote Louis Marin – 'in order to present itself in its function, its functioning, and, indeed, its functionality as representation'. As formulated and systematised in the Renaissance, the modern concept of 'representation' is coextensive with the concept of 'picture' as 'depiction'. Such a constellation of tightly interrelated notions is theoretically based on the assumption of a clear separation, enacted by a framing device, between the real world and the world of the image, as well as between perception and image consciousness.

It is precisely this separateness, and, with it, the equation of representation with depiction, that can be (and has been) challenged in two different ways. The first is to attempt to bridge the apparently unbridgeable gap between the image and actual reality. This is the subject of the second chapter of this book. The trespassing of the allegedly never-to-be-trespassed threshold established by the frame can, in turn, unfold from two different points in two opposite directions: from the image-world to the real world, or vice versa.

The first movement is paradigmatically exemplified by hyperrealistic pictures. Even though they are, indeed, the *non plus ultra* of representational images, they do their utmost to trick viewers into believing (if only for a moment) that they are perceiving reality in the flesh, not just its representation. The fusion of image and prototype can make the beholder unaware of pictorial differentiation, which is necessary for experiencing something as a representation of something else. In order to achieve maximum transparency and to convey the impression of non-mediateness, hyperrealistic pictures must dissimulate all elements that might betray their nature as representational artefacts. To be sure, frames are among these elements, for they "say" to the beholder: 'What you see in here is but an image'. Now, the objective of hyperrealistic pictures is to conceal their being pictures: they are aimed to leave the fictional dimension of representation and enter our real-life environment. To reach this goal, they must not be displayed in a context that clearly reveals what they strive to conceal, namely, their representational status. In other words, they need to be set *out of frame*.

However, crossing the borders of the frame, and thus the boundaries of representation, can also work the other way, that is, moving from the real world to (or, more precisely, *into*) the image-world. Although it proceeds in exactly the opposite direction as hyperrealistic pictures, this second movement, too, tends towards unframedness, its ultimate goal being to "pull" viewers into the image, plunging them in a new, self-consistent world. Throughout the history of mankind, the dream of immersion has resurfaced countless times, as attested by myths, legends, and science fiction narratives: from the allegory of Narcissus falling in love with his own reflection on a water surface only to drown in the attempt to reach it, to the various versions of the story of the Chinese artist penetrating into one of his pictures before disappearing within the painted landscape; from Descartes's evil genius, offering the human mind a surrogate of reality indistinguishable from actual reality, to his numerous contemporary reinterpretations, beginning with the famous thought experiment of the 'brain in a vat' proposed by Daniel Dennett in 1978, taken up by Hilary Putnam in 1981, and adapted into film by the Wachowski sisters with *The Matrix* in 1999; from *Strange Days*'s cyberpunk poetics, where people can relive the experiences of others thanks to electronic devices that record the memories and physical sensations of those who wear them, to the futuristic, unsettling universe of *Westworld*, an "amusement" park allowing wealthy visitors to spend some time in a parallel world, free to live out their most perverse fantasies courtesy of hyperrealistic androids.

Yet immersion is far from simply a matter of dreaming or imagination, as demonstrated by the stunning development of interactive virtual environments – to mention but the most recent case – that elicit in the perceiver a strong feeling of being incorporated into alternative realities characterised by the same *immediateness*, *presentness*, and *framelessness* heretofore regarded as the exclusive prerogative of flesh-bound reality. A prominent example of the potential offered by the newest technological advances has been provided by the United Nations Virtual Reality project, launched in 2015 and consisting of a series of 360-degree short films focused on various humanitarian themes. In order to explain the idea behind the project and the crucial importance of using virtual reality technology for its implementation, a few months after the first videos came out, a clip was released on the official United Nations Web TV channel entitled *Virtual Reality: Creating Humanitarian Empathy*. It begins with a rapid sequence showing images of war, epidemics, refugee crises, and natural disasters. After a few seconds, the camera pulls back to reveal these images framed on a television screen. After claiming that 'this is the way most of us are used to seeing these heart-wrenching events: on a screen in front of us, watching passively', the voice-over asks: 'What if you could step into the frame, and actually feel what it is like for the individuals on the ground?' The rhetoric of empathy, immediateness, and transparency is exploited to celebrate the immersive quality of virtual reality and to contrast it with older media, the postulate being that photography, television, and traditional cinema, forced as they are to impose a distance between the world of the spectator and the world of the image, are unsuited to letting us experience what is really going on out there, namely, beyond the frame.

Similar attempts to plunge users into virtual realities are becoming more and more popular. Although used for the most disparate purposes, they have a common trait in that they all aim to *unframe* representation, thus challenging the traditional notion of detached aesthetic experience. This "unframing strategy" found paradigmatic expression in 2017 at the 70th edition of the Cannes Festival, when Alejandro González Iñárritu surprisingly did not present a movie but an immersive installation, *Carne y Arena*. Equipped with a virtual reality headset and free to move inside a cavernous room with a sand-covered floor, the viewers, or rather the experiencers, found themselves caught up in a dramatic adventure following a group of unauthorised Mexican migrants snatched up by the United States Border Patrol while attempting a night-time border crossing. The impression of "being there", incorporated into the virtual world, is inescapable: representation is replaced by presentation, while the traditional aesthetic attitude, characterised by contemplation, detachment, and distance, gives way to immersion.

Not surprisingly, and perfectly in line with the goal of the United Nations Virtual Reality project to plunge the experiencer into the picture, Iñárritu explicitly declared his intention to break 'the dictatorship of the frame, within which things are just observed'. By literally entering the image-world, users go through a direct, first-person experience of the (re)presented events, where they feel less and less able to distinguish between the reality of the life-world and the "unreality" of the virtual world. No longer simple observers placed *in front of* images isolated from actual reality through some kind of framing apparatus, they instead become all-round experiencers placed *within* a virtual reality offering multisensory and kinaesthetic stimuli. And while *Carne y Arena* does not allow participants to do anything except move freely within its artificial environment, other simulated worlds already exist that grant users a level of interaction increasingly comparable to that of the "real world" – an expression which appears, at this point, more and more vague and almost deprived of its traditional meaning.

By making images exit their "natural habitat" and mingle with reality in the flesh, or, on the contrary, by inviting the experiencer to enter the image-world, hyperrealism and immersion proceed in opposite directions. And yet, on closer inspection, they both testify to the very same strategy of subverting representation by corroding it *from the inside*, that is, by "stretching" it to the point where it ends up negating itself and turning into presentation. Although a wax figure or an immersive virtual reality environment *are*, indeed, hyper-representational, they do their best to be *perceived* as autonomous, non-representational entities. They are both the apotheosis of representation and its *reductio ad absurdum*, for while representation implies, by definition, a mediated experience, these types of images make a semblance of non-mediateness – a semblance nonetheless achieved precisely by getting the most of the technical or technological potential of the media involved. Immersive and interactive virtual environments therefore seem to confirm what Walter Benjamin said apropos of cinema, that 'the sight of *immediate* reality has become an orchid in the land of technology'.

Trespassing the threshold of the frame is not the only way to challenge the concept, and the many different practices, of representation. As described in the last chapter of this book, a second, opposite strategy can be pursued. Rather than aiming at hyper-representation, one can strive for a *zero degree* of representation; rather than concealing the mediateness of representation, one can give it maximum visibility. In this case, paradoxically enough, the medium ceases to function as a medium: it stops mediating between the picture and its referent, thus emancipating itself from its century-old subservience to representation. Such a disentanglement of the traditional association between medium and representation brings about non-representation, just like hyperrealistic pictures and immersive environments do. Contrary to the latter, however, the exhibition of the medium is anti-representational *from the very beginning*: it does not come as a result of a process that pushes representation to its limits in an attempt to eventually turn it into presentation.

Here, representation is challenged because it is considered too illusionistic (as opposed to not illusionistic enough). Consequently, the medium is pushed not towards transparency, but towards opacity: it is *exhibited*. This exhibition undermines the whole technical and theoretical apparatus underlying the idea of representation as fiction, a concept that found its most evident expression in the traditional notion of the 'picture'. The frame is a *sine qua non* of pictorial experience: it is crucial for experiencing something as a picture-of something else that is not itself a picture.

Towards the end of the nineteenth century, this notion of the picture, and with it the common, almost taken-for-granted equation of representation to depiction, came to be regarded as no longer adequate by painters such as Georges Seurat and Claude Monet, who consequently began to question the role played by the frame in defining the fictional character of pictorial representation. The fundamental separation that all framing devices produce between the objects enclosed within them and the surrounding environment came under attack: artists dared to challenge the concept itself of the threshold of representation first by *painting* the frame, then by *reducing* it to a minimum, and eventually by completely *discarding* it. This process culminated in the work of some of the leading figures of Abstract Expressionism such as Barnett Newman, Jackson Pollock, and Mark Rothko, who all embarked on a thoroughgoing programme of un-framing aimed at ensuring continuity and coherence between the actual world and the world of the image, between reality and (alleged) unreality. If the frame provides separation, framelessness emphasises the presence of the "stripped", naked artwork in the very same spatio-temporal dimension of the experiencer.

The crisis of the easel picture, as Clement Greenberg once called it, therefore goes hand in hand with the crisis of the frame as a cornerstone of the theoretical system underpinning the modern concept of representation. This system is based on the notion of beauty as the sole and seemingly eternal ideal of art. The frame acts as a scaffolding for such an ideal. It establishes the coordinates of form, measure, and composition. It provides order and orientation. It suggests finiteness, completeness, coherence, and comprehensiveness. It sets up the Cartesian axes of simulation and fictionality. Accordingly, to remove the frame is to subvert all of these aspects of representation, replacing form with formlessness, finitude with infinitude, limitation with limitlessness – in short, beauty with the *sublime*. The transition from the frame to framelessness entails a dramatic change not only in the history of art, but also in the history of perception. As to whether this transition will (or rather *can*) ever be completed shall remain, at least in this book, an open question.

I

THE FRAME: AT THE MARGINS OF REPRESENTATION

1. *A Frame for Dubai*

Built in the sandy desert at a vertiginous speed that only petrodollars make it possible to achieve, Dubai is not simply a city; it is a symbol. A hymn to the dizzying dynamism of modern times and to the triumph of human creativity over the constraints imposed by nature, the capital of the homonymous emirate is a striking (and certainly fulsome) example of the rush for grandeur and self-purposed originality that seems to underlie the massive growth of so many contemporary metropolises. In a building frenzy of sleek residential towers, opulent offices, and shopping malls that gives free rein to futuristic projects of any kind and complexity, emblazoned starchitects have quickly succeeded in making the most famous skylines of the past century – including Manhattan's – seem like slightly retro classics.

In such a tireless quest for the extraordinary, the surprising, and the breathtaking, every opportunity is exploited to add a new entry to the book of records, starting of course with the most coveted of all its categories: the tallest building in the world. At almost 830 metres tall, more than double the height of a legendary skyscraper such as the Empire State Building, the Burj Khalifa is the undisputed lord of Dubai's landscape, dominating – both literally and metaphorically – 'The World', an artificial archipelago consisting of three hundred small islands positioned right in front of the building and designed to roughly resemble (if seen from above) the world map. Like a sovereign surrounded by his vassals, this monument to megalomania and unending ascension stands over many other super-tall skyscrapers, which, although unable to scale their superior's height, impress just as much in terms of design and aesthetic refinement: from the Emirates Towers to the Address Downtown, from the Index to the Princess, from the Burj al-Arab, whose famous "sail" stands on the artificial island of Jumeirah Beach, to the JW Marriott Marquis and the Rose Rayhaan, inevitably among the world's tallest luxury hotels. Marking yet another entry into this skyward competition, the city will soon see the completion of the Dubai Creek Tower, a minaret-shaped skyscraper designed by Santiago Calatrava whose objective is to surpass in height its Majesty, the Burj Khalifa.

In this story filled with immense wealth, towering giants of steel and glass, spectacular games of water and light, and an inexhaustible desire for self-celebration, 2008 marked an important milestone. In that year, the steel corporation ThyssenKrupp, through its Elevator division, announced the eleventh edition of its prestigious Architecture Award. With the Middle East hosting the competition for the first time, the design challenge was to embellish Zabeel Park in Dubai with 'an iconic, tall emblem structure that contributes to the new face of the city and that promotes tourism and other recreational, scientific and cultural activities'[1].

The selection committee, operating under the supervision of the International Union of Architects, were assigned the difficult task of managing 926 applications and selecting the best among them. After a first selection round, 106 projects were shortlisted and put to a worldwide online vote. By carefully examining the 62 submissions subsequently whittled down from that poll, the jury finally arrived at their decision. On 6 May 2009, the announcement was made, with the commission, including a financial prize of $100,000, awarded to Fernando Donis, a young architect and director of the eponymous architectural firm with offices in Mexico and the Netherlands.

The peculiar aim of Donis's project was to construct two parallel towers, both 150 metres high. Each would be connected at the lower and upper ends by two horizontal 105-metre corridors. Thus, the building would effectively consist of a slender hollow rectangle,

1 https://competitions.org/2008/08/thyssenkrupp-elevator-architecture-award-dubai/.

oriented in such a way as to frame the Old Town to the north (embracing the districts of Bur Dubai, Umm Hurair, Al Karama, and Deira) and the skyscrapers of new shining Downtown to the south. *To frame*: for Donis's winning project would indeed be but a gigantic frame (Fig. 1).

Fig. 1 – Fernando Donis's project for the Dubai Frame (2009)

The idea was deliberately paradoxical. Rather than building yet another monument to rival the existing massive structures whether in terms of height or sophistication of design, Donis's proposal was to make the whole city a monument *of* and *to* itself. The awesome simplicity of the 'Dubai Frame' – as the project was officially titled – was also a fundamental part of its underlying theoretical system, with its most basic geometric shape and minimalist colouring (or rather, non-colouring) perfectly reflecting the creator's intentions. Intriguingly, Donis's statement about the project represents a response both coherent with, and antithetical to, the call for tender, which explicitly required the conception of an emblem: 'Dubai is a city full of emblems. Rather than adding another one, we propose to frame them all: to frame the city. Instead of building a massive structure, the purpose of this project is to build a void. This void of 150 metres by 105 metres will continuously frame the development of the past, current, and future Dubai'[2].

To even start to consider the practical and theoretical implications of The Frame is to get lost in a maze of mirrors. What does Donis's project ultimately amount to? The first and most obvious answer must of course refer to the four-sided physical structure: its imposing materiality, dimensions, proportions, weight, and so on. Yet it is evident that Donis's Frame is not only a physical, empirical structure, but also, and above all, a *reference* structure; that is to say, a structure that, like all references, points to something other than itself. This 'other than itself' is the city of Dubai, which The Frame turns into an image of itself, with its traditional souks on one side and its distinct, 'emblematic' skyline on the other.

Things get even more complicated when we consider that this image of the city, literally *produced* by the imposing Frame, is just a snapshot (a frame, indeed) documenting a process of change that reflects the unceasing evolution of the city itself. If understood in this sense, The Frame should be compared less to the frame of a picture or photograph than to that of a screen. In other words, its counterpart is not the static image of Dubai but the spectacle of its unfolding dynamism, its metamorphosis. This spectacle constitutes the third semantic level implicit in Donis's project: what is framed and monumentalised, in this case, is not a certain portion of space, not even a specific period of time, but time as such – its passage, its flow.

The Frame, however, also consists of a fourth element, much less conspicuous than the others, but one to which the others owe their own existence: the void circumscribed by the four sides of the structure. Framing emptiness is a paradoxical operation[3]. On the one hand, the frame delimits a transparent space, thus presenting

---

2 http://donis.org/2017/?page_id=605.

3 On this, see Annette Gilbert, 'Leere Rahmen. Das Unsichtbare des Sichtbaren sichtbar machen', in *Rahmenbrüche, Rahmenwechsel*, ed. by Uwe Wirth in collaboration with Julia Paganini (Berlin: Kadmos, 2013), pp. 217–37.

itself as an outline awaiting its content, not unlike a window. On the other hand, this very same frame, since it can be filled at any given moment with unique and ever-changing content, makes this content an image. In so doing, it opacifies the surface it embraces, transforming the window into a screen.

The hard-to-decipher, provocative nature of this window-screen, which reveals its monumental character when understood as a non- or anti-monument, emerged most clearly during the project's misadventures following the announcement of Donis as the competition winner. After receiving the cash prize, the architect was invited to attend a celebration in his honour at which he got assurances that The Frame would be quickly constructed. Shortly thereafter, however, Donis received a contract that limited his role to a simple advisor, preventing him from claiming ownership of the final work. Having refused to sign it, he found himself ousted from the construction of The Frame, which was then entrusted to an external company (Al Rostamani Pegel) under the supervision of Hyder Consulting. After several failed attempts on the part of both sides to reach a satisfactory agreement, the architect was ultimately consigned to the sidelines, unable to prevent the municipality of Dubai from resolutely continuing along their path until eventually inaugurating The Frame on 1 January 2018 (Fig. 2).

Fig. 2 – The Dubai Frame (2018)

Compared to the original design, the architectural landmark underwent some significant changes: the width was reduced from 105 to 93 metres, and the simple white colour replaced by an elaborate decoration made of golden panels inspired by the logo for Expo 2020 (due to be held in the Arab emirate). Nonetheless, the underlying concept remained basically the same, which is why Donis felt entitled to sue both Dubai municipality and Thyssen at the United States Federal Court. The accusation was, of course, intellectual property infringement.

At this point, matters became even more complicated. At the end of 2016, through his trusted lawyer Edward Klaris, Donis made a formal request to protect the copyright of The Frame. Yet a U.S. Copyright Office specialist refused to register the claim on the grounds that The Frame did not appear to be an architectural work. Moreover, he maintained, even if it could be considered an architectural work, there were 'no original design elements' present that were not functionally required or that went beyond merely 'standard features'[4].

Surprised by the verdict and even more by the reasons provided, Donis appealed, replying point by point to the objections raised. In his view, The Frame should indeed have been considered an architectural work, since it was designed for human occupancy and included spaces such as cultural and conference facilities, a children's library, and a cafe. Furthermore, Donis claimed that the project was in fact copyrightable under originality standards, since, in serving as a viewing point for other landmarks in Dubai, it incorporated elements associated with form, height, and location that were *not* functionally required. The work was ultimately intended as the 'concrete manifestation of the abstract concept of a frame'.

After re-examining the case with greater attention, the Board of the Copyright Office accepted the first argument, acknowledging the architectural work status of Donis's project. However, it once again rejected the request to register The Frame as intellectual property, alleging that the structure lacked 'the copyrightable

4 This quotation and those that follow are taken from official documentation issued by the United States Copyright Office that can be accessed at: https://www.copyright.gov/rulings-filings/review-board/docs/dubai-frame.pdf.

authorship' necessary to support a registration, being nothing more than 'a very large rectangle, which is a common and familiar shape not protected by copyright'. Other factors, such as the author's inspiration, the impact of The Frame on the viewers, or the theoretical principles to which the work would give concrete form, could not be taken into consideration because, by law, those in charge of protecting intellectual property cannot formulate 'aesthetic judgments' nor consider 'symbolism or intent' in evaluating the copyrightability of particular works. Faced with this new rejection, Donis appealed again, but no changes were forthcoming, with the judgement of the Commission becoming unappealable on 29 November 2017.

The reasons behind the final decision are summarised in a statement that alone sounds like a final verdict: 'Symbolism is not copyrightable'. Relying on this assumption, the Patent Office, called upon to evaluate the originality and innovative character of a given product or project, undoubtedly carried out its mandate properly: a geometric shape placed in a public place is not, and cannot be, protected by any form of copyright. Yet the problem is that to look at The Frame as merely an artefact, evaluating it solely as a physical object, means to trivialise and ultimately misunderstand the meaning of a building whose complexity goes far beyond the building itself. If one considers its *symbolic* value (which the U.S. Copyright Office could not do), the disarming simplicity of the geometric structure no longer appears a deficiency; rather, it becomes an integral and fundamental part of the project – its veritable condition of possibility.

Indeed, Donis's Frame was conceived to divert the observer's attention away from itself and onto the city, but also onto the complex theoretical implications that both the concept of a frame and its concrete instantiation presuppose. On the contrary, The Frame built by the municipality of Dubai is a structure that attracts the gaze onto itself. It is an *attraction* in the most literal sense of the term, especially apt for framing the inevitable tourist selfies. The rich decoration and flashy colouring that are distinctive marks of the final version of the work have certainly provided it with a touch of originality, making it perhaps copyrightable. Nevertheless, upon further scrutiny, any originality it might lay claim to seems to be factitious and superficial, thus fundamentally opposed to originality proper. For, rather than accentuating the depth and complexity of the 'original' (forgive the pun) project, it in fact betrays it. As Jacques Derrida noted, 'the deterioration of the parergon, the perversion, the adornment, is the attraction of sensory matter. As design, organization of lines, forming of angles, the frame is not at all an adornment and one cannot do without it. But in its purity, it ought to remain colourless, deprived of all empirical sensory materiality'[5].

The aim of Donis's Frame was to produce an oxymoronic architecture: complex simplicity and full emptiness within a non-monumental monument. The originality of the initial idea laid precisely in its being nothing but an idea. Despite its imposing physicality, the Dubai Frame was to be understood as a purely conceptual artwork. Prevented from considering any symbolic dimension, the Copyright Office had no choice but to deliver a judgement on an extremely simple, almost banal, physical structure. However, this structure was not the real project but only its visible expression – its trigger. The quarrel between Donis and the Board of the Copyright Office thus appears to be a losing battle for both sides, a dialogue of the deaf in which the parties *cannot* reach an agreement simply because they are disputing completely different things.

Intrinsic to Donis's project was the intention to go in the exact opposite direction to everything that had been built in Dubai until then: The Frame should have been, as explicitly stated by its conceiver, an 'anti-icon'[6]. Donis would undoubtedly have been the right person to pull off such a mighty task. For eight years he had been working side by side with master architect Rem Koolhaas at the prestigious Office for Metropolitan Architecture in Rotterdam, collaborating on several anti-iconic projects specifically designed for Dubai. Perhaps the most representative of these was 'The

5 Jacques Derrida, *The Truth in Painting* (1978), trans. by Geoffrey Bennington and Ian McLeod (Chicago–London: The University of Chicago Press, 1987), p. 64.

6 Donis thus defines his work in the documentation presented to the United States Copyright Office. The same expression can also be found in the description of the project published in *Divisare*, the largest online archive specifically dedicated to contemporary architecture (https://divisare.com/projects/96251-Fernando-Donis-Dubai-Frame).

Renaissance', a Kubrickian monolithic volume made with the goal of standing out against the slender and fanciful skyscrapers of Dubai's Business Bay, an attempt to put an end to 'the current phase of architectural idolatry – the age of the icon – where obsession with individual genius far exceeds commitment to the collective effort that is needed to construct the city'. Of course, there was no more fitting city than the pearl of the Persian Gulf to stage this battle between the 'new Renaissance' advocated by Donis and an architecture in thrall to 'a mad and meaningless overdose of themes, extremes, egos and extravagance': 'Dubai is confronted by its most important choice. Does it join so many others in this mad, futile race or does it become the first 21st century metropolis to offer a new credibility?'[7]

The answer to this question posed in 2006 was to come a few years later: much to his displeasure, Donis was forced to see his Frame transformed into the umpteenth icon of Dubai. Yet his original project, too, contained an inescapable ambiguity. On the one hand, the monumental frame does what all frames do: it encourages the observer to consider the framed object *as an image*. So, what better than a monumental frame for a city that has taken image, fashion, and the triumph of appearances as its own *raison d'être*? On the other hand, however, far from distinguishing itself from the countless emblematic icons of Dubai, even the anti-icon ends up becoming nothing other than an icon: the icon of all icons. This hyper-iconic character is emphasized by the fact that The Frame, in order to actually frame Dubai, must be observed from a great distance, given that at the foot of the immense structure one would see nothing more than the frame itself, and what would be framed – and therefore transformed into an image – would only be a portion of sky. From sufficiently far away, however, the observer not only perceives Dubai framed, but also The Frame in all its magnitude, and its cumbersome shape inevitably becomes the most striking of images.

A similar feat had been previously attempted, albeit on a much smaller scale, by the Italian photographer Luigi Ghirri, who, in 1986, immortalised a supporting structure for a canopy abandoned on a beach at Marina di Ravenna (Fig. 3).

7 http://oma.eu/projects/dubai-renaissance.

Fig. 3 – Luigi Ghirri, *Marina di Ravenna* (1986)

Deprived of the curtain it was supposed to hold up, the wooden structure becomes 'a perfect picture, a frame'[8] that circumscribes a specific portion of the landscape, transforming it into an image: by framing the seashore, it makes a picture of it. At the same time, however, the frame is itself part of the landscape and, as such, it is in turn framed by the photographer's lens, which makes it an image of an image, an image raised to the second power. With this *mise en abyme* of the framing performed by the wooden frame through the framing performed by the camera, Ghirri, just like Donis, invites us to meditate on the enigma of representation or, more precisely, on the enigma of the frame as an essential element of the dispositif of representation: 'Everything you see only exists within a frame. Even the sea: how could I photograph it without framing it like a painting? If you will, it is like a window from which you look at certain phenomena; you are like a child who has

8 Luigi Ghirri, *Lezioni di fotografia*, ed. by Giulio Bizzarri and Paolo Barbaro, with a biographical text by Gianni Celati (Macerata: Quodlibet, 2010), p. 164.

to write a report on what he sees. You look out of the window, but who is actually looking? I remember a quote from a novel by Italo Calvino: "It is the world that looks at the world"'[9].

2. *Gaze-Orienting Devices*

Both the Dubai Frame and Ghirri's wooden structure are frames, but not in the most common sense of the term: they do not frame *pictures*. In this book, however, 'frame' is understood in a much wider sense: the focus is not so much on what a frame *is* but on what a frame *does*. The point is not the frame as an object, but the frame as a device, or more precisely: the frame as an essential part of the dispositif of representation (of which *pictorial* representation is simply a particular subset). In this sense, the picture frame is only a specific, albeit certainly emblematic variant of what Louis Marin defined the 'operators' and 'processes' of framing[10]. What counts most is not the frame but the gesture or 'principle'[11] of framing: the fact that, in Derrida's words, 'the frame labours [*travaille*]'[12], its work consisting in expressing, in "saying" (we will soon see how and in what sense) the representational character of the framed object. We shall then focus on framing as a 'generator'[13] of representational images.

9 Luigi Ghirri, *Il profilo delle nuvole. Immagini di un paesaggio italiano*, texts by Gianni Celati (Milan: Feltrinelli, 1989), p. 7 (October 6th).

10 Louis Marin, 'The Frame of Representation and Some of Its Figures' (1988), in *On Representation*, trans. by Catherine Porter (Stanford: Stanford University Press, 2001), pp. 352–72 (p. 353). On Marin's analysis of framing devices, see Markus Klammer, 'Kommentar zu *Der Rahmen der Repräsentation und einige seiner Figuren* von Louis Marin', *Zeitschrift für Medien- und Kulturforschung*, 7, 1 (2016), 99–108. Victor Stoichita has also called attention to the 'structural consubstantiality' between the picture frame and all other kinds of framings; cf. Victor I. Stoichita, *The Self-Aware Image: An Insight into Early Modern Metapainting* (1993), new, improved, and updated edition, trans. by Anne-Marie Glasheen, with an Introduction by Lorenzo Pericolo (London–Turnhout: Brepols, 2015), p. 90.

11 Hilde Zaloscer, 'Versuch einer Phänomenologie des Rahmens', *Zeitschrift für Ästhetik und allgemeine Kunstwissenschaft*, 19 (1974), 189–224 (p. 191).

12 Derrida, *The Truth in Painting*, p. 75.

13 Stoichita, *The Self-Aware Image*, p. 80.

Note the choice of the term *images*, not (necessarily) *artworks*. The performative nature of frames has traditionally been investigated in relation to the medium of painting, but this does not mean that it should remain confined to this field. In an essay from the early twentieth century, Gilbert K. Chesterton meditated on the ability of the frame to transform the enclosed object into a picture: 'Has not every one noticed how sweet and startling any landscape looks when seen through an arch? This strong, square shape, this shutting off of everything else is not only an assistance to beauty; it is the essential of beauty. The most beautiful part of every picture is the frame'[14]. Hugo Marcus made the same point when he pointed out that, while visiting a church, one can easily observe that people seem to 'turn into images as soon as they happen to find themselves under the nave, the arcade, or even an aedicule, a niche, or a chapel'. Similarly, the vault of an avenue of trees instantly confers 'an image character [*Bildcharakter*] to anyone passing underneath':

> How can we explain the particular iconic beauty of such scenes of real life? It is nothing more than the product of a perfectly, or even just partially, geometric framing. [...] Indeed, the frame conveys beauty even if it is not of a regular shape: the simple fact that it circumscribes a given object is in itself sufficient to guarantee its beautifying power. The more marked the closure, the greater the number of different and even opposite things that can be assimilated and transformed into an image.[15]

Here, the aesthetic force of the frame (its 'beautifying power') is overshadowed by its far more general 'iconising' quality, that is, its ability to turn the framed object – whatever it may be – into an image, into an *eikon*. Even a portion of nature or a scene from everyday life tend to assume a different value as soon as they are seen within (or through) a frame. Pietro Aretino wrote about this in a famous letter to Titian dating back to 1544. On a gloomy day, placing his arms 'on the window frame [*sul piano de la cornice*

14 Gilbert K. Chesterton, 'The Toy Theatre', in *Tremendous Trifles* (1909) (Mineola–NewYork: Dover, 2012), pp. 176–84 (p. 183).

15 Hugo Marcus, 'Rahmen, Formenschönheit und Bildinneres', *Zeitschrift für Ästhetik und allgemeine Kunstwissenschaft*, 8 (1913), 73–93 (p. 90).

de la finestra]' to contemplate the Grand Canal in Venice and the 'magnificent sight' of a fleet of gondolas, he had the impression of looking at a painting rather than a real scene: the sky seemed to him 'marvellously painted with so many shadows and lights', while the houses (*casamenti*), though built of stone, appeared to be made of 'an unreal substance [*materia artificiata*]'[16]. The terms used conjure up an almost dreamlike experience in which reality turns into an image, while the image becomes the only reality. What makes this experience possible is the window, or rather the window *frame*: Aretino 'would probably never have been able to picture the Venice sky "like Titian" had he been in the middle of a street or canal'[17]. For nature to be perceived as a painting there must be a caesura, a cut from the everydayness and "fleshiness" of the real world. This is precisely what all frames do: they perform a cut by standing in between the life-world and the world of representation.

This in-betweenness is where the frame exists – an ambiguous place, home to 'all the aporias that the notions of margin, limit, and threshold bring with them'[18]. An enigmatic 'no man's land'[19], the frame seems to be external to the framed image and yet, in a certain sense, also consubstantial to it, as an integral part of the dispositif of representation. Being *both* part of the surrounding environment and part of the iconic device, while at the same time *neither* a thing nor an image, the frame is where 'both' and

16 Pietro Aretino, *Lettere sull'Arte*, ed. by Ettore Camesasca, 2 vols. (Milan: Edizioni del Milione, 1957), II, pp. 16–18.

17 Stoichita, *The Self-Aware Image*, p. 74.

18 Antonio Somaini, 'La cornice e il problema dei margini della rappresentazione', *Le parole della filosofia* 3 (2000), 1–12 (p. 5), http://www.lettere.unimi.it/Spazio_Filosofico/leparole/duemila/ascorn.htm. For an overview of the notions of frame and framing from a multisicplinary perspective see Paul Duro (ed.), *The Rhetoric of the Frame: Essays on the Boundaries of the Artwork* (Cambridge: Cambridge University Press, 1996); Werner Wolf and Walter Bernhart (eds), *Framing Borders in Literature and Other Media* (Amsterdam–New York: Rodopi, 2006); Hans Körner and Karl Möseneder (eds), *Rahmen – Zwischen Innen und Außen: Beiträge zur Theorie und Geschichte* (Berlin: Reimer, 2010); Thierry Lenain and Rudy Steinmetz (eds), *Cadre, seuil, limite. La question de la frontière dans la théorie de l'art* (Bruxelles: La lettre volée, 2010).

19 Louis Marin, 'Les combles et les marges de la représentation', *Rivista di estetica*, 25 (1984), 11–33 (p. 13).

'neither' dialectically turn into one another[20]. It is 'something strongly "a-topical"'[21], since it stands out from both the visual object enclosed within it and from the surrounding milieu like a figure on a ground, while at the same time it also merges into each of these domains, either to define the framed object as a picture or to indicate where the milieu outside the picture begins.

Both outside and inside, the frame is neither simply outside nor simply inside, 'like an accessory that one is obliged to welcome on the border, on board [*au bord, à bord*]. It is first of all [*d'abord*] the on (the) bo(a)rd(er) [*à bord*]'[22]. With these words, Derrida alluded to a further oxymoronic characteristic of the frame, namely the fact that it counts as a sort of *necessary ornament*. Kant (whom Derrida directly refers to) had already defined the picture frame as a classic example of *parergon*, that is, an accessory merely added to the *ergon*, to the artwork proper[23]. Yet this seemingly superfluous supplement proves to be a necessary complement as soon as one realises that the artwork "proper", in order to be apprehended as such, *needs* a frame that integrates the dispositif of representation by clearly marking the threshold between the life-world and the world of the image, and by directing the viewer's gaze to the latter.

At its purest, the frame *indicates*: it is 'a deictic, an iconic "demonstrative": *this*'[24]. The group of semiologists working under the collective pseudonym 'Groupe µ' have extended the notion of 'frame' to account for the broader concept of 'border', defining it as an artifice that, in a given space, designates an iconic statement *qua* organic unity. The meaning of this sign can be summarised in three principles: '(a) A border gives all that is

20 On this, see Andrea Pinotti, 'La cornice come oggetto teorico', in *La cornice. Storie, teorie, testi*, ed. by Daniela Ferrari and Andrea Pinotti (Milan: Johan & Levi, 2018), pp. 51–67.

21 Tomáš Jirsa, 'Lost in Pattern: Rococo Ornament and Its Journey to Contemporary Art through Wallpaper', in *Where Is History Today? New Ways of Representing the Past*, ed. by Marcel Arbeit and Ian Christie (Olomouc: Palacký University, 2015), pp. 101–19 (p. 107).

22 Derrida, *The Truth in Painting*, p. 54.

23 Cf. Immanuel Kant, *Critique of Judgement* (1790), trans. by James Creed Meredith, ed. by Nicholas Walker (Oxford: Oxford University Press, 2007), p. 57.

24 Marin, 'The Frame of Representation and Some of Its Figures', p. 357.

enclosed within it a semiotic status; (b) the set of signs enclosed within a border constitutes a homogeneous statement, which is essentially different from the statements that can be perceived in the space outside the border; (c) the viewer's attention must focus on this set of signs'[25].

Accordingly, the frame is to be thought of first and foremost as a device that invites viewers to focus their gaze and attention on what is framed. In 1977, on the occasion of the sixth edition of the Kassel 'documenta', the Haus-Rucker-Co group of architects and designers presented a square structure of 14 metres per side positioned on a panoramic terrace halfway between the Fridericianum Museum and the Orangerie, where once stood the Auetor, a monumental gate dismantled in 1907 to make way for the Staatstheater, which would later be destroyed in the bombings of 1943. The name of the artwork, 'Rahmen-Bau [*Frame Construction*]', left no room for interpretation: its steel structure must only be understood as a gigantic frame (Fig. 4).

Fig. 4 – Haus-Rucker-Co, *Rahmen-Bau*, Kassel, 1977

25 Groupe μ, 'Sémiotique et rhétorique du cadre', *La part de l'œil*, 5 (1989), 115–31 (p. 115).

The choice of location was no coincidence. Panoramic vantage points allow the eye to roam free, providing an unobstructed view. At liberty to wander in any direction, the gaze automatically searches for a foothold, a landmark on which the eye can rest, an 'attractor'[26]. Once found, the observer's attention focuses on that specific point, thus drastically narrowing the perceptual field. The Rahmen-Bau is exactly this, a 'gaze-orienting device [*Vorrichtung zur Blicklenkung*]'[27]specifically designed to illustrate the functioning of perception. The imposing frame attracts the viewer's gaze and directs it towards a specific portion of the landscape, inviting the eye to stop and linger on the framed space.

Within this space, supported by a twenty-or-so-metre metal arm, is a second, smaller frame (2.80 x 2.80 metres), aptly entitled 'Landscape in a Slide [*Landschaft im Dia*]'. Thanks to a metal walkway positioned on the left side of the work, visitors can reach this structure that makes their gaze focus on the Orangerie Palace, whose baroque style contrasts sharply with the skyline of factories and industrial chimneys circumscribed by the larger frame (Fig. 5).

Fig. 5 – Haus-Rucker-Co, *Rahmen-Bau: Landschaft im Dia*, Kassel, 1977

26 Claudia Müller, *Beobachtungen am und über den Rand hinaus* (Hamburg: Hochschule für bildende Künste Hamburg, 2007), p. 113.

27 This is the definition of Rahmen-Bau that appears on the 'documenta' official website: https://documenta-historie.de/en/artworks/rahmenbau.

Both frames select portions of reality and excise them from the rest, transforming the landscape into a sort of landscape painting, albeit an ambiguous one. For, in this case, the space and time of the framed object, unlike what happens with proper pictures, are *our own* space and time. This ambiguity becomes even more conspicuous as soon as we walk towards the second frame and literally *enter* the image we had just been contemplating through the larger frame, invading the iconic space enclosed by the Rahmen-Bau and becoming an integral part of it. The observer turns into the observed.

The framed landscape is the same in which the viewer moves, both spaces belonging to the same dimension, to the same reality. And yet that portion of the landscape, for the simple fact that it is framed, takes on a radically different character with respect to the surrounding environment, even if it is, indeed, part of that very same environment. This is because the frame invites the viewer to consider what has been cut out as something special that requires attention and a specific mode of apprehension, *isolating* it from its surroundings. Unsurprisingly, the island is one of the most popular metaphors for describing frames and framing operations.

3. *Islands of Unreality*

The examples discussed so far, from the Dubai Frame through Ghirri's photograph to the Rahmen-Bau, show that the frame is to be considered first and foremost as a device for orienting the gaze towards a specific point. This also applies to the traditional picture frame, whose primary task – besides obviously protecting the framed object and making it easier to move it from one place to another – is to confer unity and coherence on the portion of space enclosed within it, while at the same time directing the observer's gaze towards it. The German term for the act of framing, *Einfassung*, indicates that the frame invites the observer to apprehend (*fassen*) what is framed as a single whole (*Eins*), as a coherent, self-sufficient, *organic* unit. In this sense, towards the end of the eighteenth century, German essayist Karl Philipp Moritz had already investigated how the frame functions in terms of the isolation of the image: 'The beauty of the frame and the beauty of the picture proceed from one and the same principle.

The picture presents [*darstellt*] something complete in itself; the frame encloses once again that which is complete in itself'[28]. Some decades later, the great architect and architectural theorist Gottfried Semper similarly defined frames (not only picture frames, but also door and window frames) in terms of 'eurythmic enclosures':

> The frame is one of the most basic forms in art: no enclosed image without a frame [...]. *Eurythmy* comes into play only when a frame is used: a regular concentric articulation and order of elements that form an enclosed figure around the framed object'.[29] [...] Thanks to this enclosure, the frame is able to transform whatever it contains into a 'microcosm'.[30]

The frame's ability to give the framed image (and, more specifically, the work of art) individuality and organic unity was then emphasised by Friedrich Theodor Vischer in 1897: 'All things that are part of ordinary reality are connected to one another. [...] Beauty instead lies in the isolation [*herausschneiden*] of the object from the infinite multiplicity of things. That's why we draw a line. A frameless picture is not likeable: it needs an enclosure'[31].

This idea that images (especially *artistic* images) are autonomous organisms separated from ordinary reality provides the starting point for Georg Simmel's famous essay *The Picture Frame*, published in 1902. Unlike the real environment in which it is placed, where each thing is nothing more than 'a transitional point for continuously flowing energies and materials, [...]

28 Karl Philipp Moritz, 'Zufälligkeit und Bildung vom Isoliren in Rücksicht auf die schönen Künste überhaupt' (1789), in *Schriften zur Aesthetik und Poetik*, ed. by Hans Joachim Schrimpf (Tübingen: Max Niemeyer, 1962), pp. 116–17 (p. 116). On Moritz's notion of frame see Till Dembeck, *Texte rahmen. Grenzregionen literarischer Werke im 18. Jahrhundert* (Berlin–New York: de Gruyter, 2007), pp. 242–94.

29 Gottfried Semper, *Style in the Technical and Tectonic Arts: or, Practical Aesthetics* (1860–1863), trans. by Harry Francis Mallgrave and Michael Robinson, intro. by Harry Francis Mallgrave (Los Angeles: Getty Research Institute, 2004), p. 86.

30 *Ibid.*, p. 404 (translation modified).

31 Friedrich Theodor Vischer, *Das Schöne und die Kunst. Zur Einführung in die Aesthetik* (1897), ed. by Robert Vischer (Stuttgart–Berlin: Cotta, 1907), pp. 116–17.

significant only as an element of the entire natural process', an artwork is 'a whole for itself, not requiring any relation to an exterior, spinning each of its threads back into its own centre'. The boundaries of a framed image signify the 'absolute ending which exercises indifference towards and defence against the exterior and a unifying integration with respect to the interior in a *single* act'[32]. The frame therefore performs a double function: it focuses the viewer's gaze and attention on what is enclosed within it, while at the same time excluding the external environment as something foreign and incompatible. The role of the picture frame lies in 'assisting and giving meaning'[33] to the inner unity of the picture as well as to the caesura that keeps it separated from external reality: synthesis and antithesis, two sides of the same coin.

Simmel points out that the isolating function of the frame can and should be reinforced by significant details: its outer sides should be higher than its inner sides, so that the four sides form converging planes that direct the gaze towards the centre of the painting[34], while the presence of two mouldings – one along the internal border, the other along the outer – helps to make the frame look 'like a stream between two banks'[35]. With the island metaphor, Simmel focuses on the frame's enclosing function, by which it acts as a 'border guard of the picture'[36], separating the world of the image from the real world. Toward the end of the essay, however, he admits that the frame not only isolates the work from the surrounding environment but, paradoxically enough, it also places the former *in relation* to the latter: 'The work of art is in the actually contradictory position of being supposed to form a unified whole with its surroundings, whereas it is itself already a whole. In this way, it repeats the general difficulty of life that the elements of totalities nevertheless lay claim to being autonomous

32 Georg Simmel, 'The Picture Frame: An Aesthetic Study' (1902), trans. by Mark Ritter, *Theory, Culture & Society*, 11 (1994), 11–17 (p. 11).

33 *Ibid.*, p. 12.

34 Moritz had already made a similar point in his *Vorbegriffe zu einer Theorie der Ornamente* (Berlin: Karl Massdorff, 1793, p. 6), arguing that the frame must 'expand externally in order that we may as it were gradually peer into the inner *sanctum* which glimmers through this enclosure'.

35 Simmel, 'The Picture Frame', p. 12.

36 *Ibid.*, p. 15.

totalities themselves'[37]. From this perspective, one can appreciate the essentially *dialectic* nature of the frame: it isolates the image – producing on the one hand a synthesis of the elements internal to it, and on the other an antithesis between the image itself and its surroundings – while at the same time connecting it to the environment. In short, the frame acts by 'separating and connecting'[38]. But how to explain the seemingly oxymoronic nature of an element that isolates while also linking, that creates a gap between two worlds while also bridging the very same gap?

To answer this question, we need to examine a different but equally crucial aspect of the island metaphor. We have so far focused on the frame as a tool for directing the observer's gaze onto the framed object, the eye being *physically* brought to linger on the framed portion of space. This gaze-focusing ability, understood in a purely material sense, certainly produces the experience of a limit, boundary, or threshold between the space within the frame and the space outside of it. But it is not in itself sufficient to isolate the former from the latter and to produce the radical, ontological fracture that separates the world of representation from the world of life. In order for such a break to occur, the viewer's gaze must not only be *physically directed* towards the space circumscribed by the frame, but it must also adopt a special *attitude*.

José Ortega y Gasset, whose seminal work is fundamental to a philosophical conception of the frame, clarifies what this particular attitude is. His *Meditations on the Frame*, written in 1921, begins with a thesis that we should by now be familiar with, namely, that the frame transforms whatever it embraces into an image:

> A picture without a frame has the air about it of a naked, despoiled man. Its contents seem to spill out over the four sides of the canvas and dissolve into the atmosphere. By the same token, the frame constantly demands a picture with which to fill its interior, and does so to such an extent that, in the absence of one, the frame will tend to convert whatever happens to be visible within it into a picture.[39]

37 *Ibid.*, pp. 16–17.

38 *Ibid.*, p. 17.

39 José Ortega y Gasset, 'Meditations on the Frame' (1921), trans. by Andrea L. Bell, *Perspecta*, 26 (1990), 185–90 (p. 187).

This is basically Marcus's thesis concerning the alleged power of any kind of framing device to turn the framed object into an image. However, one must be careful not to oversimplify this concept, for framing alone, as Ortega points out, is not sufficient to 'convert whatever happens to be visible within it into a picture'[40]. Indeed, if we were to look through a window, it would be most uncommon to register the scene outside as an image, for in most cases it would simply appear to us as external space, contiguous and akin to internal space. In the same way, if we were to see a frame exposed in a carpenter's shop, we would hardly consider the bare wall beneath it as an image. In both cases, there is no trace of a radical caesura between the domain of representation and that of actual reality.

Clearly enough, the island metaphor should not be understood solely in a material sense, and this is where Ortega's essay proves enlightening. Although the Spanish philosopher reiterates that the frame directs the observer's gaze and attention to what is contained within it, he is also keen to emphasise that this is not the frame's main ability. When looking at a picture (but also, more generally, at any framed object), one immediately notices that it requires a specific attitude, different from the one required by ordinary reality. Consider a painted, photographed, or filmed chair: not only can we not sit on it, to even try to do so is futile, because in the image world 'everything is pure metaphor, everything enjoys a merely apparent existence'[41]. The image has its own reality, which, when compared with that of the life-world, can only appear as an enigmatic unreality (or irreality):

> When I look at my grey, domestic walls, my attitude is inevitably one of vital utilitarianism. When I look at the painting, I enter an imaginary space and adopt an attitude of pure contemplation. Wall and painting, then, are two antagonistic and uncommunicative worlds. My spirit leaps from reality to unreality as if from wakefulness to dreams. The work of art is an imaginary island that floats surrounded by reality on all sides.[42]

40 *Ibid*, p. 187.
41 *Ibid.*, p. 188.
42 *Ibid.*

The clear suggestion is that the function of the frame is not to simply separate the image from the surroundings, but to isolate it in a far more radical sense, which does not relate to the physical object but to how the subject experiences it. The frame 'suspends our natural attitude towards the visual world'[43], acting as a *decontextualising device* that creates a gap and establishes a caesura within its own context. It can be counted among the main means of 'making special'[44], since it confers a unique and literally extra-ordinary character on whatever it embraces, inviting the observer to adopt an attitude radically different from that of everyday life – an attitude Ortega defines in terms of *contemplation*. Most significantly, the word comes from the Latin *templum*, which means the area of sky or land demarcated and consecrated by the augur for the taking of auspices. According to Servius (*ad Aen.* I, 446), *templum* is the same word as the Greek *temenos*, from *temno*, 'to cut off'. To con-template something is to circumscribe – that is, to frame – a certain surface from the field of the visible in order to endow it with a special significance, to "consecrate" it. In a way, the 'sacred precinct of art'[45] re-enacts and refunctionalizes the sacred enclosure of the *templum*[46].

By way of example, say we want to hang a painting. To us, the picture is an object like any other in the room. We have to take its measurements, choose the right colour for the frame, select the appropriate nail and affix it to the wall. Once this work is done, we can easily ascertain whether the painting is straight

43 Paul Crowther, *Phenomenology of the Visual Arts (Even the Frame)* (Stanford: Stanford University Press, 2009), p. 55.

44 Ellen Dissanayake, *Homo Aestheticus: Where Art Comes from and Why* (Seattle–London: University of Washington Press, 1995), pp. 39–63.

45 Julius von Schlosser, 'Dialogue About the Art of Portraiture' (1906), trans. by Karl Johns, *Journal of Art Historiography*, 5 (2011), 1–18 (p. 3).

46 On this, see Daniel Arasse, *Histoires de peintures* (Paris: France Culture–Denoël, 2004), pp. 63–64; Louise Charbonnier, *Cadre et regard : Généalogie d'un dispositif*, preface by Jean-Claude Soulages (Paris: L'Harmattan, 2007); Filippo Fimiani, 'Une esthétique imperceptible', *Figures de l'art*, 1 (2009), 217–37; Mauro Carbone, 'Thematizing the "Arche-Screen" through Its Variations', trans. by Marta Nijhuis, in *Screens: From Materiality to Spectatorship – A Historical and Theoretical Reassessment*, ed. by Dominique Chateau and José Moure (Amsterdam: Amsterdam University Press, 2016), pp. 62–69.

or crooked, whether it has been positioned in the centre of the wall or is, perhaps, slightly askew. Now, in all these operations, the picture is seen as a mere *thing*, as nothing more than a physical object.

From a phenomenological standpoint, the intentional correlate of this thing is *perception*, whose fundamental characteristic is presentation, that is, 'the exhibition of the properties of an object or of multiple objects occupying the same environment as the observer and existing in the same timeframe in which her perceptual operations unfold'[47]. As a perceived thing, the picture forms a complete and coherent sense-unit with the surrounding environment, since every single phenomenal content is part of a continuous, unitary flow, confirming preceding contents and anticipating subsequent ones.

A perceived object is therefore regarded as *actual* and *real*. Perception works like an articulate and meaningful proposition in which every single word is linked to the words that come before and those that come after. Antithetically, "disjointed" discourse is inconsistent, incoherent, devoid of logic and structure. In the same way, surprise results from something that seems out of joint with the perceptual process and that therefore demands a partial adjustment (if not a complete change) of the perceptual process itself.

Let us return to our picture. We now have it hanging on the wall, set straight and occupying its true centre. We lay down our tools and take a few steps back before finally sitting down to contemplate the mounted work. But what exactly are we 'contemplating'? Certainly not the picture as a thing, as a physical object with its own weight and dimensions; rather, it is the *image* that attracts us – and that cannot be construed as sharing the same room with us. The image-object actually marks a radical discontinuity of meaning in relation to the wall and the surrounding space. It is not part of the real and actual present both because it is not an object existing in the same environment as the observer, and because it does not fit into the coherent process that is the objectual connection characteristic of perception – and only this connection is what we call reality.

---

47 Carmelo Calì, *Husserl e l'immagine* (Palermo: Aesthetica, 2002), p. 35.

If we want to check whether the painting is straight, we must observe it in relation to the wall, *together* with it, as a physical thing next to other physical things. But if we want to contemplate the image, we of course immediately realise that the image-object and the wall belong to two fundamentally different dimensions. The objects surrounding the painting and what the painting represents are extraneous to each other. The insularity that distinguishes the image-object from any real object is already clearly marked by the edges of the painting, for those margins are also borders or thresholds: on the one side, there are things to be perceived; on the other, images to be contemplated. The frame seems to say: 'Up to this point, but not beyond it'. Rather than separating two contiguous regions of the same world, it divides two *essentially* different worlds: the real and the imaginary, each with its own space and temporality, each requiring a specific mode of apprehension.

While isolating its content from any external element, including the viewer, the frame invites this very same viewer to "enter" the framed space by crossing the threshold that keeps the reality of the life-world separated from the quasi-reality of the image world. To do so, however, the viewer must necessarily abandon the field of ordinary perception and assume an attitude of contemplation: once framed, a given object 'becomes something else, that is, a signifier, an object of art, of admiration, of interrogation. [...] Imaginary and symbolic values are added to the real. When the painter puts his brush on the canvas, he leaves, in a sense, *signs to be divined*'[48]. It is precisely by virtue of the isolation enabled by the frame that the viewer is positioned 'at that distance from which alone the picture is aesthetically enjoyable'[49].

'Distance' is the key word. The image, and with it, authentic aesthetic enjoyment, depend on keeping the necessary distance between physical space and iconic space, between reality and "unreality". To quote Moritz Geiger, another phenomenologist who provided memorable insights on the relationship between distance and aesthetic enjoyment, 'while aesthetically enjoying a painting, a landscape, a human body, a poem, or a symphony,

48 Charbonnier, *Cadre et regard*, p. 30 (emphasis added).
49 Simmel, 'The Picture Frame', p. 11.

there is always a distance between the contemplating I and the contemplated object'[50]. Years later, Giovanni Piana would reiterate the point with powerful brevity: 'Distance from the original is inherent in the very notion of representation'[51].

In developing this thesis, both Geiger and Piana were obviously indebted to the founding father of phenomenology, Edmund Husserl. Meditating on the nature and function of framing, Husserl draws the same parallel as Leon Battista Alberti between the frame and the window: 'The frame is in the visual field. It frames the landscape, the mythological scene, and so on. We look through the frame, as if through a window, into the space of the image, into the image's reality'[52]. The phenomenological window, though, is a window *sui generis*, for unlike ordinary windows it does not offer spatio-temporal continuity between the inside and the outside. The air you breathe at home is the same as the air outside; the "air" of the image is of a completely different nature. Eugen Fink, Husserl's beloved disciple, considered the window to be 'nothing but a metaphor [*nur ein Gleichnis*]'[53], since in the real world external space and internal space are on the same level, whereas the image and its medium imply mutually inconsistent space and time.

By comparing the image to a window, both Husserl and Fink aimed to highlight that the essence of every image is to manifest in the real world while at the same time marking a radical discontinuity with respect to this very same world. But in what sense is the image 'unreal'? Taking up the phenomenological metaphor of the frame as a window, Ortega defined painted canvases as 'portholes of ideality which are perforated in the

50 Moritz Geiger, 'Beiträge zur Phänomenologie des ästhetischen Genusses', *Jahrbuch für Philosophie und Phänomenologische Forschung*, 1 (1913), 567–684 (p. 632).

51 Giovanni Piana, *Elementi di una dottrina dell'esperienza. Saggio di filosofia fenomenologica* (1979) (Milan: Cuem, 2005), p. 89.

52 Edmund Husserl, 'Phantasy and Image Consciousness' (1904–1905), in *Phantasy, Image Consciousness, and Memory (1898–1925)*, trans. by John B. Brough (Dordrecht: Springer, 2005), pp. 1–115 (p. 50). The translation will be modified whenever deemed appropriate.

53 Eugen Fink, 'Vergegenwärtigung und Bild. Beiträge zur Phänomenologie der Unwirklichkeit', *Jahrbuch für Philosophie und phänomenologische Forschung*, 11 (1930), 239–309 (p. 308).

mute reality of the walls', 'openings of illusion', 'apertures of unreality'[54]. Similarly, Fink described his work as a contribution to the 'phenomenology of unreality'[55]. Yet he was also eager to clarify that the 'unreality' of the image should not be interpreted as the opposite of 'reality', given that it does not allude to a non-reality, but rather to a peculiar form of reality: 'The "unreality" of the image world [...] is an actual semblance [*wirklicher Schein*]'. He further added, in brackets: 'The word "semblance" is here not to be understood as "deception [*Täuschung*]", but rather in the same sense as we define art as a world of semblances'[56]. This is a crucial point: the unreality of the framed object should not be understood in a negative sense, for the image does not lack reality. Rather, it has its own specific reality, an oxymoronic 'unreal reality', or: a *Scheinwirklichkeit*[57], the reality of semblance. In stating that we do not react to a painted scenery in the same way we would to its real-life counterpart, Ortega is on the same page as Husserl and Fink: 'The bridge isn't really a bridge, nor is the smoke smoke, not the countryside countryside'[58]. In other words, the (un)reality of the image is a *quasi*-reality, in the etymological sense of the word: it is the reality of *quam si*, of as-if. The painted landscape is not a real landscape, but we react to it *as if* it were real, while never forgetting – not even for a moment – that we are after all dealing with nothing but an image.

4. *The Presentation of Representation*

As shown above, the frame does not simply attract the gaze toward what it circumscribes; it also clarifies what kind of gaze it invites. Not only does it say: '(Look at) this!'; it also specifies: '*This* has the reality of unreality, the reality of as-if, of making-believe – and it demands to be experienced as such'. In a letter dated 1642

54 Ortega y Gasset, 'Meditations on the Frame', pp. 188–89.
55 This is the subtitle of 'Vergegenwärtigung und Bild'.
56 Fink, 'Vergegenwärtigung und Bild', p. 306.
57 Willi Warstat, 'Der Bilderrahmen. Ein Kapitel angewandter Ästhetik', *Zeitschrift für Psychologie und Physiologie der Sinnesorgane*, 45 (1907), 441–52 (p. 441).
58 Ortega y Gasset, 'Meditations on the Frame', p. 188.

addressed to Cardinal Richelieu's minister and artistic consultant Sublet de Noyer, Nicolas Poussin described two different ways of perceiving objects:

> One is simply to see them [*aspect*], the other to consider them attentively [*prospect*]. Simply to see [*aspect*] is nothing other than to receive naturally in the eye the form and the resemblance of the thing seen. To consider it attentively [*prospect*] means that beyond the simple and natural reception of the form in the eye, one takes special pains to find a way to know that same object well: thus we may say that simple 'aspect' is a natural operation, and that what I call 'prospect' is an office of reason.[59]

In this passage, Poussin draws a clear distinction between two kinds of gaze. While 'aspect' refers to naturally functioning vision, 'prospect' (from the Latin *prospectus*, meaning a panoramic view, a vision from a distance) implies a rational operation that results in a theoretical-contemplative gaze. By delimiting, focusing, and de-contextualising *both* the image *and* the viewer's gaze, the frame causes a switch from *aspect* to *prospect*, from seeing to contemplating (contemplation being the attitude peculiar to aesthetic enjoyment). The gesture of framing activates that 'modalisation of the gaze'[60] which is required to access the domain of representation. And 'required' must be here unequivocally understood as follows: a certain modification of the gaze is a *necessary condition* for representation to take place.

In its various historical forms, the frame has always determined 'the grammar and pragmatics of the gaze'[61] that addresses the framed image: it dictates the conditions that give access to the world of representation. In other words, the frame neutralises the claim to reality of the surrounding environment. By isolating the representational space from ordinary reality, it also isolates *iconic* apprehension from *perceptual* apprehension. Commenting on Poussin's correspondence, Marin does an admirable job of explaining and further developing the concept: the frame

59 Nicolas Poussin, 'Correspondance', ed. by Charles Jouanny, *Archives de l'Art français, Nouvelle période*, 5 (1968), p. 143.
60 Marin, 'The Frame of Representation and Some of Its Figures', p. 357.
61 Somaini, 'La cornice e il problema dei margini della rappresentazione', p. 1.

'transforms the varied play of perceptible diversity, the raw material of the perceptual syntheses of recognition of the things that articulate them by way of differences, into an opposition in which representation is identified as such through the exclusion of all other objects from the field of the gaze'[62]. The modalisation of the *gaze* is understood here as a modalisation of *consciousness* that intends the framed object. The opposition Poussin established between *aspect* and *prospect*, between the ordinary gaze and the rational one, is translated into an opposition between perceptual synthesis and imaginative synthesis.

The terms used by Marin are clearly phenomenological, as is the entire theoretical scheme that makes the frame an essential part of the dispositif of representation. Hardly surprising, then, that the phenomenological movement's leading figure had some important observations of his own to make on the nature and functions of the frame. Husserl takes his cue from a distinction between two different modes of apprehension: in *perceptual* apprehension (*Wahrnehmungsauffassung*), the intended object appears directly in itself, whereas in *pictorial* apprehension (*Bildauffassung*) it appears indirectly, namely through a picture. In perception, the object appears to us 'in its own person, as it were, as present itself'[63]. In pictorial consciousness, on the contrary, the object still appears, but not as something present, for it is only 'presentified [*vergegenwärtigt*]': 'It is as though it were there, but only as though'[64]. Only in perception is the object taken for real. Perceptual consciousness therefore requires not only that the object appears 'in person [*leibhaft*]'[65], but also that it is meant as real. The object that appears in pictorial consciousness is instead not the object itself but a 'representative' of it, a *Stell-Vertreter*, something that, literally, 'takes the place' of something else.

62 Marin, 'The Frame of Representation and Some of Its Figures', p. 356.

63 Husserl, 'Phantasy and Image Consciousness', p. 18.

64 *Ibid.*

65 Edmund Husserl, 'Vitality and Suitability in Re-Presentation; Empty Re-Presentation. Internal Consciousness, Internal Reflection. The Strict Concept of Reproduction' (1911–1912), in *Phantasy, Image Consciousness, and Memory (1898–1925)*, pp. 363–74 (p. 367).

Husserl gives the example of a photograph portraying his child[66]. In addition to the physical thing (*Bildding*) perceived, namely the photographic paper *qua* physical substrate of the image, the intentional acts involved in pictorial consciousness imply a 'double objectivity'[67]. First, there is the image-object (*Bildobjekt*), i.e. the miniature child, which appears due to the organisation of perceptual data provided by the medium (the photographic paper) and as a result of the observer giving it a coherent meaning. Second, there is the image-subject (*Bildsujet*), that is, Husserl's child in the flesh, to whom the image analogically refers. This *sujet* is, by definition, absent, being only 'presentified' through the representational reference.

In short, two different acts overlap within pictorial consciousness, since the very same material of sensation undergoes two different apprehensions, being intended either as the perceptual qualities of the *Bildding*, or as the iconic qualities of the *Bildobjekt*. And this 'either... or' is for Husserl mutually exclusive: there is *either* a perceptual apprehension of the physical thing *or* an iconic apprehension of the image-object in its referring to the image-subject. In a landscape painting, for instance, purely perceptual content is 'everything we see in the painting, yet without the representational reference to a landscape'[68]. We can concentrate on the canvas, on the pigments, on the pattern the painter has arranged them in. But in doing so, we lose sight – even if only momentarily – of the represented image. For it to appear, perceptual appearance must be "replaced" by pictorial appearance. The intermingling (*Durchdringung*) of the physical thing and the image-object goes hand in hand with a conflict (*Widerstreit*) in their apprehension modes[69], meaning that apprehension of the

66 Edmund Husserl, 'Phantasy and Image Presentation' (1898), in *Phantasy, Image Consciousness, and Memory (1898–1925)*, pp. 117–51 (p. 118).

67 *Ibid.*, p. 121.

68 Piana, *Elementi di una dottrina dell'esperienza*, p. 87.

69 On this, see Eduard Marbach, *Mental Representation and Consciousness: Toward a Phenomenological Theory of Representation and Reference* (Dordrecht–Boston–London: Kluwer, 1993), pp. 126–36.

image-object pushes apprehension of the physical thing 'into the background of consciousness'[70].

Husserl makes here a very similar point to Simmel's. When we contemplate the iconic world represented in a picture, its physical substrate is not what we dwell on; however, the picture itself belongs to a real context that can, indeed, be perceived *together* with it. In other words, the physical image certainly contributes to 'the more comprehensive unity of the objective apprehension'[71]. Yet, on closer inspection, we actually notice that 'not the whole picture but only certain of its components (the framing [*Umrahmung*]) are woven into the unitary surroundings of the depicted object and thus brought to objective apprehension with it'[72]. It is often said that pictorial objects seem to emerge from the frame or that, on the contrary, the frame appears as a window through which we can penetrate the iconic space. This suggests that the real world and the image world are linked together to form one coherent objective set, a single cohesive present. Yet in fact this unitary connection of reality and pictoriality does not concern the whole picture as a physical thing, only its frame.

Indeed, the apprehension of the image *qua* image deprives the apprehension of the image *qua* physical thing of its contents. The apprehension contents of the *Bildding* now function as the apprehension contents of the *Bildobjekt*. In pictorial consciousness, the physical thing coincides with the image-object: it is 'covered' by it and 'disappears' behind it. What does not disappear, 'in the unitary apprehension pertaining to the visual field'[73], is the frame, which relates both to the dispositif of representation *and* to physical reality.

Husserl leaves no doubt that the frame is not part of representation. Regardless of how far consciousness intending its object may extend beyond the apprehended objectivity, the pictorial representation 'nevertheless finds no support in that

70 Edmund Husserl, 'Modes of Reproduction and Phantasy Image Consciousness' (1912), in *Phantasy, Image Consciousness, and Memory (1898–1925)*, pp. 401–82 (p. 419).

71 Husserl, 'Phantasy and Image Presentation', p. 134.

72 *Ibid.*

73 *Ibid.*, p. 49.

apprehension of the frame'. This is because the frame exercises no representational function:

> If, as is most natural, we restrict the talk of pictorial representation to the act that turns toward a represented object and means it, the just-described partial participation of the physical image thing in the pictorial representation does not come into consideration at all. Only what functions representatively, or is constitutive of what represents, belongs to it.[74]

At the same time, however, the frame is an integral part of the *dispositif* of representation, as it stands, and mediates, between the life-world and the image world: it is, literally, the "intermediary" of representation[75]. Prompting the observer to 'bracket' the natural world (*a parte obiecti*) and its assumed perceptual apprehension (*a parte subiecti*), the frame gives access to the imaginary dimension that is the hallmark of representation: it is part of the dispositif of as-if. A framed picture is isolated from ordinary reality, but ordinary reality is only given by the observer's 'gaze' or, phenomenologically put, by the observer's mode of apprehension. Changing the gaze (that is, switching from one mode of apprehension to another) allows the observer to be "in tune" with the framed image, thus enabling the communication between the real world and the world of representation which is the yardstick of aesthetic enjoyment. In this sense, frames may be understood as 'objectifications of the aesthetic attitude'[76].

Therefore, the frame does not represent: rather, it presents the representation. It signifies both the transparency and opacity of representation, its being similar to, and *at the same time* inevitably different from, what is represented. The ambiguity typical of the frame – its fundamental in-betweenness – is the ambiguity of representation itself. If 'to represent means to present oneself representing something'[77], the frame is the middle term: it is the

---

74 *Ibid.*, p. 134.

75 Jacques Aumont, *L'œil interminable : cinema et peinture* (Toulose: Seguier, 1989), p. 111.

76 Karsten Harries, *The Broken Frame: Three Lectures* (Washington, DC: Catholic University of America Press, 1989), p. 67.

77 Marin, 'The Frame of Representation and Some of Its Figures', p. 352.

link (and not just the 'isolator', as postulated by Ortega)[78] between presentation and representation, between the life-world and the image world. As 'the empirical moment of an ideal or essential operation of constituting a perceived object as a theoretical object'[79], the operation of framing is essential to the dispositif that every representation must include 'in order to present itself in its function, its functioning, and, indeed, its functionality as representation'[80].

78 Ortega y Gasset, 'Meditations on the Frame', p. 189.
79 Louis Marin, 'The Frame of Representation and Some of Its Figures', p. 425, n. 26.
80 *Ibid.*, p. 353.

II

INSIDE AND OUTSIDE THE FRAME: HYPERREALISM AND IMMERSION

1. *Like a Drawbridge*

We have seen that one of the main functions of frames consists in isolating the image from the surrounding environment, marking a radical discontinuity between the world of life and the world of representation. This *objectual* discontinuity goes hand in hand with the different modes in which these two worlds are *subjectively* apprehended: on the one side, there is perception; on the other, quasi-perception or pictorial consciousness. The frame therefore invites the observer to adopt the correct attitude in front of the picture and to take part in the play – a term we will soon come back to – of representation.

In the general context of the meaning and power of framing operations, works of art have always provided a paradigmatic (though certainly not exclusive) example of this kind of double isolation. The need for a sharp separation between the reality of ordinary things and the (un)reality of representation (more specifically, of artistic representation) was particularly emphasised, once again, by Georg Simmel, who warned about the potential 'danger' that a picture could blend into its surroundings, incapable of standing out 'with sufficient independence'[1]. To avoid this risk, the frame should never offer 'a gap or a bridge through which, as it were, the world could get in or from which the picture could get out – as occurs, for instance, when the picture's content extends into the frame, a fortunately rare mistake, which completely negates the work of art's autonomous being and thereby the significance of the frame'[2]. Here, rather than

1 Simmel, 'The Picture Frame', p. 13.
2 *Ibid.*, pp. 12–13.

an island, the frame appears as a moat, filled with water, surrounding a castle. Indeed, the island and the sea are connected to each other, water and land blending together at the seashore's boundaries. The moat, instead, standing *between* the walls of the fortress and the surrounding land, seems to better symbolise the liminal space proper to the frame.

About ten years before Simmel wrote his famous essay, another German scholar had focused on the isolating and "defensive" function of frames, making some fundamental observations that anticipated many of the topics that would be addressed by later critics throughout the twentieth century and up to the present day. Yet, unlike Simmel, Konrad Lange – whose contribution can be defined, without exaggeration, as the first systematic analysis of the frame as an integral part of the dispositif of representation – has been, and continues to be, completely ignored by scientific literature on this field.

A professor of Art History at the University of Tübingen, Lange lay the foundations for his theoretical building in an essay dated 1895, *Conscious Illusion as the Core of the Enjoyment of the Arts*. The starting questions of the paper are: what do different forms of art have in common? What makes them all, indeed, *art*? Traditional aesthetics answered by invoking the concept of 'beauty', which, however, proved to be too vague to serve as an effective criterion for understanding the specificity of the artistic domain. After all, a fascinating natural spectacle, a person's soul, or even a particularly elegant scientific demonstration can all be described as beautiful.

What Lange proposes is a completely different solution. He takes the marble group of the *Wrestlers*, kept in the Uffizi, and compares it with two wrestlers in the flesh, who practice an art form (a 'martial' art) which, as such, can certainly be enjoyed aesthetically. But why, Lange wonders, is aesthetic enjoyment fundamentally different, and way more intense, in the case of the artwork? Why is it that 'although common sense suggests that reality is worth more than its reproduction, in this case we have greater joy in front of the copy than the original? [...] Because thanks to phantasy we turn dead marble into people of flesh and blood'[3].

3 Konrad Lange, *Die bewusste Selbsttäuschung als Kern des künstlerischen Genusses* (Leipzig: Veit, 1895), p. 9.

According to Lange, the enjoyment that springs from contemplating a sculpture does not derive from the object considered in its materiality but from the psychic act that animates it. This is not an intellectual act, but a sentiment, a *sich einfühlen* – a way of empathising with, and getting inside, the bodies and their movements: the *Wrestlers* are represented 'as if they were not inanimate statues but living beings'[4]. Of course, we can also identify and empathise with the real wrestlers, but that would be a quite different kind of identification, based on a merely sensory act rather than on imagination. Only a work of art can disclose the imaginative dimension of simulation and pretence by which we act *as if* the world of fiction were real, *as if* the world of representation were a world made of 'flesh and bone'[5].

Here we come to the crucial point of Lange's conception, which amounts to a psychological aesthetics based on the notion of *illusion*. A work of art is everything that allows for, or rather requires, a certain attitude: the attitude of 'as if', defined by Lange as a 'conscious illusion [*bewusste Selbsttäuschung*]'. The notion first appeared in a book from 1893 devoted to *The Artistic Education of German Youth*, where the author identified the true essence of artistic enjoyment as the 'animation of iconic semblance [*Scheinbildes*] by means of phantasy' or, in other words, as a 'conscious and voluntary illusion' based on 'constant oscillation between semblance and reality'[6].

Yet, how can illusion be conscious? If illusion, by definition, lasts only until we realise that we have been deceived, then how can we fall into an illusion while at the very same time being conscious of it? Lange's idea – important aspects of which had already been anticipated in the nineteenth century by Jean-Baptiste Du Bos and

4 *Ibid.* On the concept of empathy with particular reference to psychological aesthetics see Andrea Pinotti (ed.), *Estetica ed empatia* (Milan: Guerini, 1997).

5 Here I can only cursorily mention the fact that the recent discoveries of the so-called mirror neurons and of embodied simulation have instead questioned this distinction between body simulation and imaginative simulation, also with reference to the specific field of artistic fiction.

6 Konrad Lange, *Die künstlerische Erziehung der deutschen Jugend* (Darmstadt: Bergsträsser, 1893), pp. 21–22.

Moses Mendelssohn[7] – is that 'artistic' or 'aesthetic' illusion is an essentially different phenomenon from illusion as it is commonly understood, that is, a perceptual deception that only lasts until we realise we have been tricked. As soon as we become aware of this, perceptual illusion vanishes: 'It is of the nature of illusion not to present itself as such'[8]. On the contrary, *aesthetic* illusion lies in being tricked while perfectly knowing that the trick is nothing but a play, the play of representation. Artistic illusion is to be interpreted in the etymological sense of *in-lusio*, a term that alludes to *ludus*, to playfulness, to 'playing along' and acting *as if*.

This explains why, according to Lange, there is a constitutive, *genetic* link between children's play (in particular, symbolic or 'pretend' play) and artistic representation. A child pretending that a broomstick is a horse is perfectly aware – and, importantly, *perceptually* aware[9] – of the fact that the broomstick is not 'really' a horse, just as anyone contemplating van Gogh's sunflowers knows (and is perceptually aware) that they are not 'real' sunflowers. It is *as if* the broom were a horse; it is *as if* that tangle of lines and colours were a sunflower. What play and art share is precisely the imaginative dimension of the 'quasi', of the *quam si*: a quasi-horse, a quasi-sunflower, an 'intertwining of semblance and truth'[10] that harbours the very essence of the enjoyment of art and play. In both cases, something has to *act as* the image of something else: the child looks for an object that meets the minimum requirements to be acted as a horse, while the painter seeks the mechanisms to conjure up – to quote Ernst Gombrich, a careful reader of Lange's work – 'a convincing image despite the fact that not one individual shade corresponds to what we call "reality"'[11].

---

7 Cfr. Jean-Baptiste Du Bos, *Critical Reflections on Poetry, Painting, and Music* (1719), trans. by Thomas Nugent (New York: AMS, 1978); Moses Mendelssohn, 'On the Main Principles of the Fine Arts and Sciences' (1757), in *Philosophical Writings*, trans. and ed. by Daniel O. Dahlstrom (Cambridge: Cambridge University Press, 1997), pp. 169–91.

8 Maurice Merleau-Ponty, *Phenomenology of Perception* (1945), trans. by Colin Smith (London–New York: Routledge, 2013), p. 295.

9 See Alberto Voltolini, 'Visually-Based Knowingly Illusory Presence and Picture Display', *Phenomenology and Mind*, 14 (2018), 158–68.

10 Lange, *Die bewusste Selbsttäuschung*, pp. 22–23.

11 Ernst Gombrich, *Art and Illusion: A Study in the Psychology of Pictorial Representation* (1960) (Princeton–Oxford: Princeton University Press,

Thus, the illusion described by Lange and Gombrich has nothing to do with a more or less perfect imitation of 'reality' (tellingly, in the above-quoted sentence, Gombrich puts the term in quotation marks). Instead, aesthetic illusion is the ability to find – or rather to produce – *analogies* between actual reality and the reality of representation. We act as if the broomstick were a horse, as if the drawing were a sunflower, but without ever confusing the first term of the analogy with the second. Finding analogies means being able to notice similarity *in difference*: being conscious of the gap between the image and its referent is a necessary condition of analogy, and therefore also of representation. In other words, there need to be elements that prevent aesthetic illusion from turning into perceptual illusion.

In this regard, Lange introduces the notion of 'anti-illusionistic moments [*illusionstörende Momente*]'[12], meaning all elements that prevent any form whatsoever of actual deception. And this is where the frame comes into play: 'By enclosing the picture within a frame, the painter seems to want to say: "What I am offering you is not nature but art. My paintings are not intended to deceive you, but to invite you to play the game of illusion [*einer spielenden Selbsttäuschung*]"'[13]. It is important to note that this invitation to 'play the game' of representation comes from *all* kinds of framing: pedestals underneath sculptures, theatre stages, and television screens have the same function as picture frames, exemplifying what Quatremère de Quincy called the 'charm-dispelling instruments that apprise the viewer of the fiction and its artifice'[14].

2000), p. 49.

12 Lange, *Die bewusste Selbsttäuschung*, p. 20.

13 Konrad Lange, *Das Wesen der Kunst: Grundzüge einer realistischen Kunstlehre*, 2 vols (Berlin: Grote'sche Verlagsbuchhandlung, 1901).

14 Antoine Chrysostome Quatremère de Quincy, *An Essay on the Nature, the End, and the Means of Imitation in the Fine Arts* (1823), trans. by J.C. Kent (London: Smith, Elder & co., 1837), p. 148. In the very same paragraph, de Quincy also links together the picture frame and aesthetic illusion: 'When the painter includes within a narrow compass a vast extent of space, when, on a flat surface, he bears me through the far-off regions of the infinite, and makes the air and light appear to circulate around forms devoid of relief, I find delight in abandoning myself to his illusions. But nevertheless I would not have the frame absent; I would wish to know that what I see is in fact but a piece of canvas, or a perfectly plane surface' (p. 147).

In other words, they count as an essential part of the dispositif of representation and, as such, require viewers to adopt a specific, contemplative, or playful attitude.

In what is arguably his *magnum opus*, *The Essence of Art*, Lange further develops the topics he had introduced previously in his essay on conscious illusion, this time insisting on the importance of the frame as an essential element of aesthetic experience. The first edition of the work, published in 1901, clearly delineates the role of framing in establishing a difference between modes of apprehension. The argument is similar, but not identical, to the one proposed in 1895: 'By enclosing the work within a frame, the painter seems to want to say: "What I am offering you is not the work of nature, nor is it one of those things you can perceive [*sehen*] in the surrounding environment: it is instead the work of an artist, a work that requires being contemplated [*angeschaut*] and enjoyed [*genossen*]"'[15]. Here we find the double isolation produced by the gesture of framing, a matter that would subsequently be tackled by all scholars who take an interest in the role of the frame as a means for presenting representation: on the one hand, there are ordinary things and perception; on the other, there are images, contemplation, making as-if, and aesthetic enjoyment. As Marin would put it about eighty years later, 'there we looked at the world, at nature; here, we are contemplating the work of art alone'[16].

In the second edition of *The Essence of Art*, published in 1907, Lange employs the metaphor of the island to describe a difference both in terms of objective contents (real things vs images) and of modes of apprehension (perception vs contemplation). Thanks to the frame 'the artwork is isolated [*isoliert*], separated from the surrounding environment, marked as an artefact. This is critically important for aesthetic intuition [*ästhetischen Anschauung*]'[17].

At this juncture, things may seem rather confusing. On the one hand, Lange claims that it would be 'completely mistaken'[18] to state that the frame enhances the illusion. On the other hand, however, we have seen that the frame itself can be understood –

15 Lange, *Das Wesen der Kunst* (1901), I, p. 210.
16 Marin, 'The Frame of Representation and Some of Its Figures', p. 357.
17 Konrad Lange, *Das Wesen der Kunst: Grundzüge einer illusionistischen Kunstlehre* (Berlin: Grote'sche Verlagsbuchhandlung, 1907), pp. 222–23.
18 *Ibid.*, p. 223.

especially in relation to a picture painted according to the canons of classical perspective – as a powerful 'generator of spatiality [*Raumschöpfer*]'[19], a window opening onto the pictorial space and inviting the observer to come inside. As noted by Hilde Zaloscer, this produces, indeed, a high degree of illusionism. This seeming contradiction can be reconciled by clarifying the terminology used. If by 'illusion' we mean 'perceptual deception', then the frame is, indeed, a strongly anti-illusionistic element. On the contrary, if we mean 'aesthetic illusion', then the frame can certainly contribute to increasing the illusionistic effect of a painting[20].

In short, aesthetic illusion is based on what Samuel Taylor Coleridge called a 'willing suspension of disbelief'[21]. Indeed, it is precisely the concept of 'belief' that allows one to distinguish between the two types of illusion. Unlike perceptual illusion, aesthetic illusion does not admit belief. The German word for 'perceiving' is *wahr-nehmen*, which literally means 'taking for real'. In phenomenological terms, perceptual consciousness is therefore always a *positional* consciousness. Perceiving something, as such, implies that the perceiving subject believes that the perceived object exists: to quote Merleau-Ponty, perceiving 'is placing one's belief in a world'[22]. Existence-belief counts as an essential part of the perceptual phenomenon: perception is essentially thetic, which means that there can be no such thing as genuine perceptual experience without belief-character. On the contrary, in pictorial consciousness the subject takes no position on the reality of the

19 Zaloscer, 'Versuch einer Phänomenologie des Rahmens', p. 200 and p. 203.

20 As Karsten Harries pointed out, the frame raises 'an aesthetic barrier that protects the artificial world created by the painter from the reality beyond and thus protects our collusion with the artist's fiction. To do so, it may not absorb too much of our attention. It should attract it only to send it on, should invite us to look past the frame, pass through it, into the picture. If the frame in this sense invites us to become absorbed in the picture, it also shadows such absorption with an awareness of the illusory character of the world of the picture, of its distance from the real world' (*The Broken Frame*, p. 68).

21 Samuel Taylor Coleridge, *Biographia Literaria* (1817), ed. by James Engel and Walter Jackson Bate, 2 vols (Princeton: Princeton University Press, 1985), II, 6.

22 Merleau-Ponty, *Phenomenology of Perception*, p. 297.

image-object, which, strictly speaking, is not 'perceived', in the sense that it is not taken for real (*wahr-genommen*).

To shed light on this difference, we can usefully refer to a distinction made by Husserl between *Wahrnehmung* and *perceptio*. The very use of the Latin term gives evidence to the great difficulty of describing a mode of perceptual apprehension that, unlike perception proper (that is, perception as *Wahr-Nehmung*), does not imply any position-taking in relation to the actual existence of the intended object. In short, Husserl uses *perceptio* to describe a situation where the subject, despite grasping an object through sensory intuition, does not ascribe actual reality to it.

By virtue of the anti-illusionistic moments that necessarily characterise images *qua* images, pictorial enjoyment turns out to be a mode of apprehension based on *perceptio*, not on *Wahrnehmung*. And this is precisely why artistic illusion is essentially different from perceptual illusion. The latter always occurs within a positional context. I initially perceive the oasis in the desert as if it were real; as I get closer, I realise I have been deceived, and it is then – only then – that I become conscious of the illusion. What I previously considered real, now possesses 'annulled reality; that is, nullity'[23].

None of this happens when it comes to images. Art presents what Husserl defines in terms of '*ficta* consistent with *perceptio*', that is, figments or fictional objects that the observer apprehends through the senses, yet without considering them as actual reality:

> We are, of course, actually experiencing, but we are not in the attitude of actual experience; we do not actually join in the experiential positing. The reality changes into reality-as-if for us, changes into 'play'; the objects turn into aesthetic semblance: into mere – though consistent with *perceptio* – phantasy objects.[24]

Here, in the context of Husserlian phenomenology, we do find the very same parallel drawn by Lange between art and

23 Edmund Husserl, 'On the Theory of Image Consciousness and Figment Consciousness' (1912), in *Phantasy, Image Consciousness, and Memory*, pp. 581–99 (p. 581).

24 Edmund Husserl, 'On the Theory of Intuitions and Their Modes' (1918), in *Phantasy, Image Consciousness, and Memory*, pp. 599–658 (p. 615).

play. And it is no coincidence that Husserl, too, writes about the contrast between 'illusion in the ordinary sense, understood as a "semblance" to which we "succumb"', and "artistic" or "aesthetic" illusion'[25]. Nevertheless, he does not explicitly acknowledge his debt to Lange, but he merely makes a generic reference to 'sources, which do not interest us here'[26]. Still, the difference between the two kinds of illusion is described in basically the same way by both scholars: aesthetic illusion is grounded in a form of 'phantasy complying with *perceptio* [*perzeptive Phantasie*]' that is at work *from the outset*, namely, from the very first moment the perceiver starts to play the game of representation.

The frame delimits the playing field. As the Spanish word *marco* suggests, it acts as a 'marker', a 'demarcation' line between two territories, with reality on the one side, and the image (and aesthetic illusion) on the other. As already mentioned, the frame is a figure of what the Greeks called *temenos*: framing means fencing, marking a caesura between two fundamentally different fields. Unlike perceptual consciousness, pictorial consciousness is essentially analogical: it is consciousness that intends objects in the *as if* mode. In his *Logical Investigations*, Husserl notes that there are 'characteristic differences in syntheses of fulfilment' between perceptual and pictorial consciousness[27]. Perception fulfils itself 'through the synthesis of identical thinghood [*sachlichen Identität*]': the object appears 'in itself', not merely 'in a likeness'. On the contrary, imagination and pictorial consciousness fulfil themselves 'through the peculiar synthesis of image-resemblance': 'The likeness [...] is related to the thing by similarity: where there is no similarity, there can be no talk of a likeness, an image'[28].

25 *Ibid.*, p. 617.

26 *Ibid.*, p. 618. The fact that Husserl refers here to Lange's theory is also demonstrated by his criticism of those who (like Lange, indeed) believe that the aesthetic illusion consists in a continuous *oscillation* between reality and fiction, between perception and pictorial consciousness.

27 Edmund Husserl, *Logical Investigations* (1900–1901), trans. by John N. Findlay, ed. by Dermot Moran, 2 vols (London–New York: Routledge, 2001), II, p. 219.

28 *Ibid.* On this, see Valeria Ghiron, *La teoria dell'immaginazione di Edmund Husserl: fantasia e coscienza figurale nella "fenomenologia descrittiva"* (Venice: Marsilio, 2001), p. 117.

A few years later, in *Phantasy and Image Consciousness*, Husserl provides further context:

> If the conscious relation to something depicted is not given with the image, then we certainly do not have an image. This conscious relation, however, is given through that specific consciousness belonging to the re-presentation of what does not appear in what does appear, according to which what does appear, by virtue of certain of its intuitive properties, gives itself as if it were the other.[29]

Now the emphasis is on the observer's perceptual awareness of the iconic (in the sense of the Greek word *eikon*) nature of the image, i.e. of the image *qua* image-of: pictorial consciousness requires the existence of a conflict, however subtle or nuanced, between the image and its referent. And the observer must be *fully aware* of this conflict: there must be no room for doubt or hesitation in identifying the image *as an image* (and not as the "real thing").

Yet this full awareness can only take place if, beyond the general resemblance, however pronounced and accurate it may be, we can still grasp moments of dissimilarity, of difference and conflict between *Bildding*, *Bildobjekt* and *Bildsujet*. Husserl's 'moments of difference'[30] perfectly echo the 'anti-illusionistic moments' described by Lange in the very same years as the founder of phenomenology: these are the elements by which the image is recognised from the outset as an arte-fact.

But what happens if these elements fail to appear? What if the drawbridge that Simmel considered a necessary condition of all images (and hence of aesthetic enjoyment) is lowered, and the threshold separating the quasi-space of representation from the space of actual reality suddenly vanishes?

2. *Ladies and Guards*

Originally Austrian, naturalised French, Ferdinand Bac (born Ferdinand-Sigismond Bach) was the illegitimate nephew of Jérôme

---

29 Husserl, *Phantasy and Image Consciousness*, p. 32.

30 *Ibid.*, p. 44.

Bonaparte, Napoléon's youngest brother. Raised on the margins of the Second French Empire, after the collapse of the regime he decided to move to Paris, where the *prince impérial* Napoléon Eugène Louis Bonaparte (Napoléon IV for the Bonapartists) introduced him into high society. A writer, painter, cartoonist, landscape gardener, and one of the leading caricaturists of his time, the young Ferdinand led a well-off and suitably bohemian lifestyle, expanding his social circle up to include celebrities such as Victor Hugo, Paul Verlaine, Guy de Maupassant, Giuseppe Verdi and Richard Wagner, to name but a few.

Among the many exciting events of Bac's life, the one that most relates to our purposes may at first seem of minor importance. It is hidden amid the fascinating pages of his *Trip to Berlin*. After a long walk along the shore of the Spree River, Bac reaches Palais Monbijou, home to the former Hohenzollern Museum[31]. Intrigued, he walks in to visit the forty-two rooms hosting the collections of the Königliche Kunstkammer, enriched over time by a number of artefacts celebrating the glorious history of the House of Hoenzollern. Suddenly he meets 'a strange person who, sitting in an armchair next to a door, seems to be part of the surveillance staff. His sleepy look is typical of museum guards, the eyes about to close at any moment'. Dressed in outmoded clothes, with a wide-brimmed hat on his head and an ermine robe over his shoulders, 'he stands there quietly observing the visitors'. Confused, without really knowing why, Bac moves away from the guard so as to see him better before finally solving the mystery: 'So who is this bizarre man supervising the room? It is a wax statue, an impressive *trompe l'œil* in the likeness of Frederick I of Prussia'[32].

With its striking mimetic fidelity, the hyperrealistic mannequin is made to deceive the observer and conceal its true nature, hiding its being nothing but a picture. It (or perhaps, more to the point, 'he') seeks to escape the frame of representation and enter our world – the world of actual reality. To do so, it needs to blur the boundaries between the two

31 Severely damaged by bombings during World War II, the museum (or rather what was left of it) was demolished in 1959.

32 Ferdinand-Sigismond Bach, *Le voyage à Berlin : La fin de l'Allemagne romantique* (Paris: Conard, 1929), p. 51.

domains as much as possible, ridding itself of any element that could possibly unmask it as just an image. In Bac's story, it is the anachronistic clothing that betrays the 'guard', giving rise to suspicion and driving the visitor to move away and look again. This distancing re-establishes – also from a merely physical standpoint – the gap between the image-world and the world of life that the wax figure tries instead to bridge. Only due to this distance could an anonymous guard be recognised as a hyperrealistic representation of a "celebrity" who clearly, at the time of Bac's experience, was no longer famous.

This point should not be overlooked. To meet a celebrity is for most people a very rare event. The powerful, the rich and the famous are often surrounded by a particular kind of aura that seems to make them exceptionally distant even if we happen to be physically close to them. They are icons, unreachable images of themselves. Their intrinsically iconic nature is what makes them immediately recognisable, preventing them from going unnoticed. It is pretty much impossible for celebrities to blend in with the crowd and mingle with "ordinary" people. Their oft-repeated claim to privacy does not entail a desire for isolation, but the exact opposite: a desire to feel "like everybody else", if only for a while.

Bac's visit to the Hohenzollern Museum dates to 1929. More than two centuries had passed since the death of Frederick I in 1713, which explains Bac's failure to recognise the once famous monarch at first glance. Yet it is precisely this supervening anonymity that facilitates the objective of the wax statue, allowing it – if only for a few moments – to go unnoticed and blend in with the real-life guards, like a real person among other real people. Without a frame to isolate it from ordinary reality and declare it an artefact, the mannequin is an outsider to the world to which it nevertheless belongs, that is, the world of representation.

If we decide to spend a few hours at Madame Tussauds, we perfectly know what to expect. Like all museums, wax museums are also part of so-called 'institutional frames', environments that generate specific expectations. By entering a museum or an art gallery, we always cross a threshold, a line separating ordinary reality from the "unreality" (or *as if* reality) of the iconic experience: 'The ideal gallery subtracts from the artwork all cues that interfere with the fact that it is "art". The work is isolated from everything that would detract from its own evaluation of itself'[33]. Once again we return to the theme of isolation. By virtue of simply being placed within the museum frame, an object takes on a particular value, an iconic status that distinguishes it from all ordinary things.

This also applies to museums such as Madame Tussauds or Grévin, which claim no allegiance to the art world. Like all frames, they too generate expectations in the sense that we expect to find in them, if not works of art, at least *images*, i.e. representations that, as such, must reveal their iconic nature beyond (and in spite of) their astonishing realism. For this to happen, however, the image must immediately be perceived *as an image*, and the fact that it is framed within a museum helps achieve precisely this goal: 'The stability of the frame is as necessary as an oxygen tank is to a diver. Its limiting security completely defines the experience within'[34].

Yet the museum space does not fully correspond to the space of representation. The hall, the ticket office, the cafeteria, the bookshop and the toilets are all part of the same ordinary reality, having nothing to do with the quasi-reality of representation. Like Chinese boxes, museums are macro-frames including progressively smaller frames that increasingly delimit the representational space and direct both the viewer's gaze and attention toward it. The rooms of an art gallery and, within them, the many spaces specifically designed to exhibit the individual artworks and to isolate them from actual reality through barriers or dividing lines of various kinds – all serve as frames. They guide visitors by providing them with a sort of map that clearly indicates the boundaries between reality and representation.

That is what frames are: *orientation tools*. The sharper the delimitation established by the frame, the easier it is to orient the viewer's gaze. And the other way around: the more nuanced and porous the frame, the more confused and disoriented the viewer. As paradigmatically highlighted by Marcel Duchamp, an ordinary

33 Brian O'Doherty, *Inside the White Cube: The Ideology of the Gallery Space*, Expanded Edition (Berkeley–Los Angeles: University of California Press, 1999), p. 14.

34 *Ibid.*, p. 18.

object assumes an extra-ordinary value as soon as it is isolated within a frame. But what happens when, on the contrary, a framed object (therefore separated from ordinary reality) is deprived of its 'isolator' (to recall Ortega's definition) and thrown into the space-time continuum of reality in the flesh?

In 1928, a year before Ferdinand Bac visited the Hohenzollern Museum, a major intellectual of the twentieth century inadvertently came upon the answer to this question. In one of the famous pages of his autobiographical novel *Nadja*, André Breton describes his experience at the Grévin Museum. He walks in, pays for his ticket and begins the visit. Suddenly, 'between the room of modern political celebrities and that at the rear of which, behind a curtain, is shown "an evening at the theater"'[35], he notices a woman adjusting her garter in the shadows. The temptation is irresistible: after quickly ascertaining that no one is watching, Breton yields to the voyeuristic instinct and casts a fleeting glance back at the intriguing scene. Nothing has changed; everything is as before, *exactly* as before. Startled by such unnatural immobility that contradicts his perceptual expectations, he feels compelled to look again: still the same result – no movement, no change. No life. For the 'garter woman' is nothing but an 'adorable lure' purposely fashioned to deceive the visitor: it is 'the only statue', as Breton admiringly puts it, 'with *eyes*: the eyes of provocation'[36].

It is highly significant that both Bac and Breton attribute a gaze to the hyperrealistic mannequins that fool them. The saying 'the eyes are the mirror of the soul' is particularly apt, for the gaze is closely linked to life and the life-world. Directly referring to Breton's experience, Walter Benjamin believed it impossible not to lose heart in front of the unsettling 'immortalization of the ephemeral [*Verewigung des Ephemeren*]' performed by the wax lady[37]. The ephemeral is the very sign of life, inevitably subject to incessant change. The anonymous 'woman' fastening her garter is indeed caught in a moment that should remain private, away

35 André Breton, *Nadja* (1928), trans. by Richard Howard (New York: Grove Press, 1960), p. 152.

36 This expression, which appears in the original French, has been inexplicably excised from the English translation.

37 Walter Benjamin, *The Arcades Project*, B3, 4 trans. by Howard Eiland and Kevin McLaughlin (Cambridge MA–London: Belknap Press, 1999), p. 69.

from prying eyes. Unlike ordinary wax figures, she is neither exhibited nor exposed: she is not positioned *inside* a room but *between* two rooms, in a place of passage not subject to the laws of representation but to those of the real world, the world of life. As Hans Blumenberg would have it, 'wax figures do not strive to be looked at as mere pictures but as persons in the flesh'[38].

Presaging Bac, Breton, and Benjamin, Konrad Lange had previously recorded a conceptually identical experience:

> I remember a few years ago, at the top of the stairs of the Castan's Panopticon in Berlin, there was a wax lady tilting her head, bringing the *lorgnette* to her eyes from time to time, winking at the visitors coming up. Those who saw her for the first time were almost invariably deceived; then, getting closer and focusing on her movements, they realised that they had been tricked. In such cases, of course, aesthetic enjoyment goes right out the window. [...] Genuine aesthetic enjoyment can only exist when the artist gives up any form of actual deception [*wirkliche Täuschung*] from the outset, providing viewers with anti-illusionistic moments that make *conscious* illusion [*bewusste Selbsttäuschung*] arise. When viewers apprehend a work of art as a pure and simple aesthetic semblance and let themselves get caught up in the illusion *almost* to the point of mistaking the image for reality, then conscious illusion arises, and aesthetic enjoyment with it. On the other hand, when they find themselves at first deceived, and only after a while they realise they have fallen into a trap, they are left with nothing but disappointment [*Enttäuschung*], that is, a feeling of displeasure.[39]

Actual deception (perceptual illusion) necessarily leads to disillusionment, and therefore to disenchantment. On the contrary, aesthetic illusion leads to a game of analogies in which the image is recognised as such from the start. Being deprived of any kind of frame that could reveal its artefactuality, the wax figure escapes the space of representation and enters the realm of real life, thus eliciting in the observer a series of perceptual expectations that, however, are fated to remain unmatched. The woman's stillness or, perhaps, the mechanical stiffness of her

38 Hans Blumenberg, *Höhlenausgänge* (Frankfurt a.M.: Suhrkamp, 1989), p. 714.
39 Lange, *Das Wesen der Kunst* (1901), pp. 245–46.

motion; her empty gaze; her slightly unnatural skin tone: all of these aspects ultimately reveal her being nothing but the image of a real woman.

Interestingly (but, at this point, unsurprisingly), Husserl offers a quite similar description of the exact same figure mentioned in Lange's anecdote: 'I remember the scene at the waxworks in Berlin, how startled I was when the all-too-amiable "lady" on the staircase beckoned to me. But how, after somewhat regaining my composure, I suddenly recognised that this was a mannequin calculated to deceive me'[40]. These words were written in 1912, but the visit to Castan's actually dates to a time when Husserl was still a young maths student. The story, which recurs as a veritable leitmotif throughout the philosopher's corpus, was given its first airing in *Logical Investigations* between 1900 and 1901:

> Wandering about in the Panopticum Waxworks we meet on the stairs a charming lady whom we do not know and who seems to know us, and who is in fact the well-known joke of the place: we have for a moment been tricked by a waxwork figure. As long as we are tricked, we experience a perfectly good percept: we see a lady and not a waxwork figure. When the illusion vanishes, we see exactly the opposite, a waxwork figure that only *represents* a lady.[41]

Both in Lange and Husserl, the viewer's awareness of being confronted with nothing but an image is a *conditio sine qua non* of representation. This awareness is in turn based on the recognition of certain elements of difference between the image and its referent. Without this contrast, the game of representation is lost, and aesthetic illusion gives way to perceptual illusion, that is, to deception.

Yet this is precisely what the wax guard and the wax lady are: images that do everything they can to deflect recognition, images that negate themselves or, in other words, *an-icons*, a term recently introduced by Andrea Pinotti to define all images purposely made to conceal

40 Edmund Husserl, 'On the Analysis of Memory. Characterization of Internal Memory and Characterization through the Later Nexus: Omission and Supervention of Position Takings' (1912), in *Phantasy, Image Consciousness, and Memory*, pp. 497–507 (p. 497).

41 Husserl, *Logical Investigations*, II, pp. 137–38.

their true nature of images[42]. Hyperrealistic pictures count among self-negating images in that they seek to obfuscate the difference between physical thing and image object, as well as that between image object and image subject. When looking at a painted portrait of a man, we usually have no difficulty in distinguishing between the medium and the image: on the one hand, there is a framed, pigmented canvas; on the other, a face. Even when considering a photograph – the mimetic reproduction *par excellence* – the moments of difference between physical thing and image object, as well as those between the representing image and the represented *sujet*, are all too evident. The chromatic nuances, shape, and actual dimensions of the photographic paper are certainly not the same as those of the image that appears on that paper.

One might perhaps object that these are overly simplistic, non-representative examples. After all, paintings and photographs are two-dimensional objects, whereas the image objects that appear in them represent three-dimensional subjects. In principle, however, the same argument applies to busts or full-length sculptures: they are immediately recognisable as images, and it is only this recognisability that can grant them access to museums and art galleries.

As for wax figures, however, things get much more complicated. Where does the wax end and the represented flesh begin? Or, if you will, where does the physical thing end and the iconic object begin? The first is so similar to the second that it tends to overlap (and thus to identify) with it. In this sense, then, what is denied is a fundamental trait of pictorial consciousness, namely, the conflict or difference between physical thing and image object. As a result, it is no longer possible to affirm that the image appears *by means of* a physical thing, because image and thing are now (almost) perfectly superimposable.

Yet the lady and the guard do not only obliterate the difference between physical thing and image object; they also aim to annihilate the difference between image object and image subject.

42 See on this Andrea Pinotti, 'Self-Negating Images: Towards An-Iconology', *Proceedings*, 1 (2017), 1–9 (doi:10.3390/proceedings1090856), and Pietro Conte, *In carne e cera. Estetica e fenomenologia dell'iperrealismo* (Macerata: Quodlibet, 2014), pp. 32–33.

Their mimetic fidelity is too strong, too *immediate*, in the literal sense of the term: it makes the mediateness of representation vanish. But no mediateness means no image. Reflecting on the boundaries of representation, Husserl refers to the 'limit case'[43] in which the direct apprehension of the image object overlaps with the indirect apprehension of the image subject in such a perfect manner that it becomes indistinguishable from it: 'In the case of a perfect portrait that perfectly presents the person with respect to all of his moments (all that can possibly be distinctive traits), indeed, even in a portrait that does this in a most unsatisfactory way, it feels to us as if the person were there himself'[44]. Only 'as if', though, for under ordinary circumstances this 'person himself' clearly belongs to a context other than that of the image object: 'The actual person moves, speaks, and so on; the picture person is a motionless, mute figure'[45].

This is *usually* the case. Yet wax figures change the whole game, since they have the same strength, stability, and intuitive 'fullness [*Fülle*]' that we attribute to perceived objects. Thanks to mechanical devices, they can even move and utter words, thus perfectly embodying the 'limit case' mentioned by Husserl, whereby the synthesis between image object and image subject encompasses all of the moments of appearance of the former that are able to resemble the properties inferred in the apprehension of the latter. And as even the minimum degree of difference that is needed to distinguish the representing image from the represented object is lost, *similarity* becomes *identity*. In this second sense, the 'lady' denies another essential condition of pictorial consciousness, that of the 'double object': image object and image subject turn out to be indistinguishable from each other.

Wax figures are not reference structures: they are intended to *present* – rather than to *represent* – someone or something. And this is why, as long as we see the mannequin as a real person, we have an ordinary perceptual apprehension (*Wahrnehmung*), the lady being (mis)taken for a real person. Unlike the image proper, "her" space is our space, "her" time our time. "She" breathes the

43 Husserl, 'Phantasy and Image Consciousness', p. 34.
44 *Ibid.*, p. 33.
45 *Ibid.*

air we breathe; "she" exists in our same environment; "she" returns our gaze. A wax figure is the appearance of a real person:

> The consciousness of reality can be inhibited by conflict with another consciousness of reality, but it is consciousness of reality. The illusory thing [*Scheinding*] stands before me in the nexus of these physical things belonging to my surroundings, in the same space, as a thing like them, and as real as they are. The wax figure has real hair, real clothes. Everything – or almost everything – that belongs to it and appears and genuinely appears, appears with as much reality as it does in the case of other things. Only when I examine it carefully do the differences, the vacillating, and so on, emerge. In the case of the normal image, but certainly also in the case of an image object decisively distinguished from its image subject, I have no consciousness of reality at all, not even an 'inhibited' consciousness. I have no inclination whatsoever to take the image object as real.[46]

But how is it, then, that the wax statue is eventually recognised as a picture and not as a real person? How and when do we realise that we have been misled? For this to happen, the 'horizon of typical familiarity'[47] in which objects are normally perceived must start to falter. Ultimately, certain elements will seem out of

46 Edmund Husserl, 'Reproduction and Image Consciousness', Appendix L: 'On Imagination' (1912), in *Phantasy, Image Consciousness, and Memory*, pp. 569–73 (p. 480). Husserl describes the difference between a bust and a wax statue in similar terms: 'We have two spaces with different fillings that "overlap", and the things involved have nothing in common. That means that the situation is not what it is in the opposing case of an *illusion*: in the case of the mannequin/human being, for example. In that case, the mannequin has clothes, hair, which would also be the clothes and hair of the human being. Determinate properties held in common are perhaps also present in the form of the superficial properties of the hands, cheeks, and so on. What about the case of a bust? Here, to be sure, the superficial forms, but no concrete parts, no concrete physical aspects of the thing, are partially held in common. Otherwise, the situation would be what it is in the case of the panorama, and there would again be an illusion'; Edmund Husserl, 'Reproduction and Image Consciousness', Appendix LI: 'Meditation: On the Possibility of Viewing Mere Imagining as Perceptual Positing "Entirely Annulled"', in *Phantasy, Image Consciousness, and Memory*, pp. 575–79 (p. 575).

47 Edmund Husserl, *Experience and Judgment: Investigations in a Genealogy of Logic* (1948), trans. by James Spencer Churchill and Karl Ameriks, ed. by Ludwig Landgrebe (Evanston: Northwestern University Press, 1973), p. 42.

place and cause suspicion, driving us to double-check in order to ascertain how things "actually" stand. In the case of wax figures, the suspicion is usually caused by a lack of movement or – if the statue is equipped with devices enabling it to perform relatively complex gestures – its unnatural, non-human jerkiness. We can easily figure out the scene of Husserl entering the museum and heading for the ticket office, joining the queue, glancing distractedly at the flight of stairs and noticing a lady motioning him to ascend. Puzzled, he looks around to check whether he really is the object of the invitation and, seeing nobody else nearby, he turns again towards the lady. Once again the exact same gesture: the head rises and turns slightly, the bust and the arm move accordingly. *Déjà vu*.

This is when perceptual illusion begins to waver; or rather, this is when perceptual illusion *vanishes*. Because illusion always implies full belief, it does not allow for hesitation or even the slightest suspension of judgement. Unlike the appearance of the image, which clearly presents itself *as an image*, the appearance of illusion remains hidden – it is contingent on *not* being noticed. As soon as we begin to doubt its true nature, the illusion is over: 'Whether one is being the victim of illusion cannot be understood so long as one remains entangled in the illusion itself. Image consciousness, instead, is always consciousness of the image *qua* image. Strictly speaking, the semblance of illusion is always a *past* appearance ("I had fallen into an illusion"), while the semblance of the image is a *present* appearance ("I am contemplating an image right now")'[48]. As Jean Baudrillard argued, 'so long as an illusion is not recognized as an error, it has a value precisely equivalent to reality. But once the illusion has been recognized as such, it is no longer an illusion. It is, therefore, the very concept of illusion, and that concept alone, which is an illusion'[49].

48 Hans Jürgen Seemann, *Bild als Widerstreit: Zur Phänomenologie des Bildes im Anschluß an die Untersuchungen E. Husserls. Ein Beitrag zur Phänomenologie der anschaulichen Unmöglichkeit*, Dissertation vorgelegt bei Prof. Dr. Klaus Held (Gesamthochschule Wuppertal: Wuppertal, 2000), pp. 128–29 (http://elpub.bib.uni-wuppertal.de/servlets/DerivateServlet/Derivate-746/da0001.pdf).

49 Jean Baudrillard, *The Perfect Crime* (1995), trans. by Chris Turner (London–New York: Verso, 2002), p. 51.

Hyperrealistic dummies fascinate phenomenologists precisely because they allow them to investigate the relationship between image and illusion as well as that between pictorial consciousness and perceptual consciousness. The present of perception is intertwined with 'retentions' related to past experience and 'protentions' that anticipate its future course. Surprise and disorientation always stem from unmet expectations, since our belief in a world existing in itself is specifically based on these expectations and their being met. Husserl's lady challenges the consistency of experience, that is, its coherence: 'Perceptual belief loses its belief-character for a moment because it is traced back to a deceptive perception and competes with another belief'[50]. *First* it was a woman; *now* it is a mannequin.

Game over? Well, not entirely. The wax figure still has an ace up its sleeve and sticks resolutely to its task. Even when unmasked, it stays in the game: 'With its real clothes, hair, and so on, indeed, even with movements artificially mimicked by means of mechanical devices, the wax figure so closely resembles the natural human being that the perceptual consciousness momentarily prevails again and again. The imaginative apprehension is suppressed'[51]. From a phenomenological perspective, this is a crucial statement, for it implies that the issue cannot be solved by merely resorting to ontological considerations: *nothing* except a different act of consciousness distinguishes the mannequin from the real human being. Yet consciousness itself struggles in front of wax figures, indefinitely oscillating between perceptual apprehension and pictorial apprehension, thus stuck in 'a kind of "paralysis"'[52]. The excessive resemblance overshadows the "unreal" character of the image and causes the tension between presence and absence – which is inherent to the concept of representation – to slacken. The result is that even after realising that we were facing the *image* of a

50 Iris Därmann, *Tod und Bild. Eine phänomenologische Mediengeschichte* (Munich: Fink, 1995), p. 284.

51 Husserl, 'Phantasy and Image Consciousness', p. 43.

52 Rudy Steinmetz, *L'esthétique phénoménologique de Husserl: Une approche contrastée* (Paris: Kimé, 2011), p. 135. By the same Author, see also 'Les limites de la représentation visuelle. A propos du cadre chez Husserl, Merleau-Ponty et Derrida', *Alter : Revue de phénoménologie*, 15 (2007), pp. 77–101.

person, we cannot but see the *person* herself – flesh, and not wax. After temporarily replacing perceptual consciousness, pictorial consciousness must confront it again and again, imposing itself in a frantic attempt to remind us that we are in fact the victims of an illusion – wax, and not flesh.

Yet with time comes clarity. It usually takes but a few moments to realise that we have fallen into the mannequin's trap. But even so, 'we cannot help ourselves – we see a human being'[53]. This is the most relevant phenomenological datum: the ongoing mismatch between *knowing* and *seeing*. On the one hand, perceptual consciousness cannot fully take hold because of the doubt that slowly creeps in, affecting the regular course of perception. On the other hand, pictorial consciousness also fails to gain the upper hand, simply because the extraordinary resemblance of wax figures to real persons forces us to ceaselessly switch between pictorial and perceptual apprehension.

It is precisely because of the 'indecisive nature of the boundaries between the artistic and the living'[54] that wax figures fall outside the sphere of art. Like Lange, Husserl notes that being momentarily deceived by a hyperrealistic puppet is enough to prevent the viewer from experiencing any authentic aesthetic enjoyment:

> The image must be clearly set apart from reality; that is, set apart in a purely intuitive way, without any assistance from indirect thoughts. We are supposed to be taken out of empirical reality and lifted up into the equally intuitive world of imagery. Aesthetic semblance [*Schein*] is not sensory illusion [*Sinnentrug*]. The delight in blunt disappointment or in the crude conflict between reality and semblance, in which now semblance passes itself off as reality, now reality as semblance – reality and semblance playing hide-and-seek with each other, as it were – is the most extreme antithesis to aesthetic pleasure, which is grounded on the peaceful and clear consciousness of imaging. Aesthetic effects are not the effects of annual fairs.[55]

53 Husserl, 'Phantasy and Image Consciousness', pp. 43–44.
54 Ortega y Gasset, 'Meditations on the Frame', p. 189.
55 Husserl, 'Phantasy and Image Consciousness', p. 44.

Regardless of whether they are ladies or guards, hyperrealistic images are in principle *out of frame*: their goal is precisely not to be "framed" as images. Positioning them outside the ordinary exhibition spaces does nothing but make them more transgressive, accentuating their ability to *trans-gredi*, to (literally) 'overstep the boundaries', to cross the threshold of representation and become part of our world. And it is precisely this characteristic that makes them, both in Lange and Husserl, intrinsically unaesthetic.

However, when it comes to art (and, in particular, *contemporary* art), surprise is always right around the corner. And the corner is in this case the one behind the entrance to the exhibition rooms at the Nelson-Atkins Museum of Art in Kansas City, Missouri. Who is that guard looking out the window, lost in thought? Known to his fellow guards as Roy, we are in fact observing *Museum Guard*: Duane Hanson's hyperrealistic creation from 1975 (Fig. 6).

Fig. 6 – Duane Hanson, *Museum Guard* (1975).
The Nelson-Atkins Museum of Art, Kansas City, Missouri

So it *is* a work of art: a statue that, just like the fake guards and ladies we have discussed so far, seems to have been made to deceive the unfortunate passer-by. Through the use of polyester, fiberglass and vinyl, the modern heirs of wax, it too relies on an extraordinary degree of realism; it too is carefully placed outside the traditional exhibition space, allowing the visitor to approach without restriction.

Between 2011 and 2012, on the occasion of a retrospective dedicated to George Ault[56], Hanson's guard was moved to a different room from the one in which he was usually found (or rather "met"). Letting Roy "himself" explain the reasons for his temporary displacement, the museum's curators put up a sign next to the room's entrance:

> Duane Hanson's realist sculpture, *Museum Guard*, has stood faithfully at his post in Gallery L3 since the Bloch Building opened in 2007. Now that two of the contemporary galleries have been emptied to make room for the exhibition *To Make a World: George Ault and 1940s America*, he requested assignment elsewhere in the museum. 'Since my arrival at the Nelson-Atkins on November 18, 1976, I've heard only praise for the museum. Now, I have the good fortune to see what everyone has been talking about. For the next two months, I will be in this beautiful historic American home!' he said. 'Then, I will be reassigned to Gallery P24, where I will experience the elegance of 18th-century English life in the King's Lynn Room'.

This sign actually helps us to understand the difference between Roy and the fake wax guards *à la* Madame Tussauds. The clearly ironic tone of the message does not increase, but drastically reduces the 'reality effect' of the image, thus making the playful nature of the installation explicit: the curators are inviting visitors to play Roy's game. What matters most, however, is that the game is played from the very beginning, that is, from the moment one enters the Nelson-Atkins Museum. Hanson's work is part of a collection of an institution that, unlike Madame Tussauds, is an *art* museum and, as such, creates expectations different from a wax museum. What

56 *To Make a World: George Ault and 1940s America*, organized by the Smithsonian American Art Museum in Washington and hosted by the Nelson-Atkins Museum from 15 october 2011 to 8 January 2012.

makes the difference is the frame in which the work is inserted. Of course, a visitor may be blissfully unaware that Roy is a work of art, and therefore more likely to fall into the trap that has been set. Even in this case, however, another frame is provided to re-establish the correct distance between the image and reality: the caption. Providing the visitor with information on the work contributes to delimiting the field of aesthetic illusion as opposed to that of actual deception.

As Gombrich notes, labelled wax figures housed in galleries 'are "portraits of the great". The figure on the staircase made to hoax the visitor simply represents "an" attendant, one member of a class. It stands there as a "substitute" for the expected guard'[57]. The Nelson-Atkins guard, though, is no longer just *a* guard: he is *the* guard created by Duane Hanson, he is Roy – an ordinary man turned celebrity. The fake guard of wax museums, just as Rudolf Arnheim argued, is not intended 'to interpret the nature of their fellow guards but to increase weirdly the staff of the institution'[58]. Revealing himself as a work of art, instead, Roy invites us to reflect precisely on the guard's "nature", on his existential condition, on his humanity – a topic central to Hanson's artistic vision. It could therefore be said that among the many meanings that can be associated to Museum Guard, there is an ironic and yet serious problematisation of the relationship between Madame Tussauds-style hyperrealism, which only aims at escaping the frame of representation, and another type of hyperrealism that manages instead to rise above simple technical virtuosity and imitation for its own sake by expanding the frames of art in new and unexpected directions. Let us see how.

3. *Framing, Reframing*

It is a well-known maxim that the meaning of cultural objects 'depends on the context' in which they are embedded. Images

---

57 Ernst Gombrich, 'Meditations on a Hobby Horse or the Roots of Artistic Form' (1951), in *Meditations on a Hobby Horse and Other Essays on the Theory of Art* (Oxford: Phaidon, 1963), pp. 1–11 (p. 3).

58 Rudolf Arnheim, 'The Robin and the Saint: On the Twofold Nature of the Artistic Image', *The Journal of Aesthetics and Art Criticism*, 18, 1 (1959), 68–79 (p. 72).

are no exception. In order to interpret their value and function properly, we must be able to 'contextualise' them correctly, so that they can "speak" their own language and express what they have to "say". However, this seemingly intuitive idea is often completely misunderstood, due to the belief that it is possible to 'reconstruct' the context (allegedly the only, true, immutable context) on the basis of objective criteria that make it possible to discard all forms of hermeneutical arbitrariness. This is the powerful legacy of a misinterpreted positivist approach that, after stretching Leopold von Ranke's famous dictum that history should be told 'the way it happened [*wie es eigentlich gewesen*]'[59], made it the banner of a "scientific" historiography based on purely empirical data, facts, and events, meant as something to be *explained* [*erklärt*] rather than *understood* [*verstanden*]. From this perspective, to reconstruct the context means to eliminate (or at least to attempt to eliminate) any trace whatsoever of the interpreter's subjectivity.

Yet such an approach has proved to be not only utopian but also conceptually wrong: utopian, because both in the so-called hard sciences and in the humanities that alleged objectivity has always been, and always will be, a chimera, since the "filter" of subjectivity is not only a constitutive and unavoidable part of experience, but also its condition of possibility; conceptually wrong, because that objectivity is not even desirable, since the achievement of an "ultimate" and absolute objectivity would mean the end of cultural objects *tout court*. Indeed, the condition for something to be called a *cultural* object is that it actively contributes to determining the given context (as opposed to being merely part of it), doing so – and this is the fundamental point – again and again. The context does not consist of a 'self-evident, non-conceptual kind of data'[60], but is itself a cultural product, and like all cultural products it is in constant transformation. This means that new ways of reading a "fact" or a set of "data" necessarily imply a re-modulation of the context, which is modified *après-coup* by the interpreter.

59 This expression appears in the famous preface to *Geschichten der romanischen und germanischen Völker von 1494 bis 1514* (1824), in *Leopold von Rankes Sämmtliche Werke*, 54 vols (Leipzig: Duncker & Humblot, 1867–1890), XXXIII (1874), p. VII.

60 Mieke Bal, *Travelling Concepts in the Humanities: A Rough Guide* (Toronto: University of Toronto Press, 2002), p. 134.

Alongside (or in some cases instead of) the notion of context, cultural studies have thus begun to focus on *framing*. Employing this concept is not merely a terminological choice, for it entails a radical change of perspective:

> Context is primarily a noun that refers to something static. It is a 'thing', a collection of data whose factuality is no longer in doubt once its sources are deemed reliable. 'Data' means 'given,' as if context brings its own meanings. The need to interpret these data, mostly only acknowledged once the need arises, is too easily overlooked. The act of framing, however, produces an event. This verb form, as important as the noun that indicates its product, is primarily an activity. Hence, it is performed by an agent who is responsible, accountable, for his or her acts.[61]

In short, a 'given' set of data is actually never 'already given', and the interpreter does not just find it there, ready to be interpreted. The subject's task is not – and *cannot* be – to let data speak for themselves, simply because data, on their own, will inevitably remain silent. The point is not to *reconstruct the one right* context, but to *construct a possible* context by organising – that is, by framing – certain "data" in a certain way. The notion of framing presupposes not only that there is no absolute truth, but also that there is no absolute context: the act of framing is what *creates* the context, and data become such only when they are framed by an interpreter. Thus, while the notion of context refers to an immutable entity that should be reconstructed step by step, detail after detail, by the historian, the concept of framing harbours the idea of a work in progress, a perennial metamorphosis: the emphasis is on cognition as an activity, as an ongoing process, as *time*.

And with time comes change. Cultural analysis treats its objects as living beings that assume their distinctive appearance and meaning only over time and only based on the different ways in which they are constantly framed and reframed. This applies in particular to images:

> 'Framing' questions the object-status of the objects studied in the cultural disciplines. This questioning results in a repositioning of the

61 *Ibid.*, p. 135.

> object as alive, in ways that have to do with the 'social life of things' rather than with a metaphysical hypostatizing of objects or a rhetorical strategy of personification. It also results in the status of image – rather than text – as the most characteristic, indeed, paradigmatic, kind of cultural object, provided we continue to see it as living its life in the present and the ways we frame it as provisional.[62]

Framing is an activity, a hermeneutical performance that *creates* its own objects, which live only *in* and *through* that performance. The meaning, or rather, the meanings of cultural objects should not be sought in an imaginary "original context", but in the relations that the objects themselves establish with the present of the interpreter, that is, of the "framer". From this point of view, frames are not only material structures made to outline and circumscribe images, but also instruments that perform a specific task: the task of framing.

Meant as cultural objects and, therefore, liable to be framed in ever-changing ways, images describe trajectories that can lead the observer to give them a meaning different from, or even opposite to, the author's original intentions. And this ongoing process of framing and reframing is a fundamental, unavoidable part of the life of the images themselves. The complex interactions between reality and the multifarious imageries in which reality itself is framed make it possible for images to convey different meanings, thus proving that their aesthetic and semantic value is in constant evolution. The act of reframing 'brings out possible meanings in an image that one did not think of before it was reframed in this way. This act is the opposite of historical interpretation. [...] Analysing the way images are, and have been, framed helps to give them a history that is not terminated at a single point in time, but rather continues; a history that is linked by invisible threads to other images, the institutions that made their production possible, and the historical position of the viewers they address'[63].

Let us consider a concrete example. *Lunch Atop a Skyscraper* is one of the most famous images in the history of photography.

62 *Ibid.*, p. 137.

63 Mieke Bal, *Reading Art*, in *Generations and Geographies in the Visual Arts: Feminist Readings*, ed. by Griselda Pollock (London: Routledge, 1996), pp. 25–41 (p. 33 and p. 41).

It shows eleven workers on their lunch break seated on a metal girder, their feet dangling two hundred and fifty metres above the streets of New York. When it was published in 1932, the photograph immediately became the icon and advertisement for the revival of the United States after the "Great Crash" of 1929 and the ensuing global economic crisis. Although a small element, the girder was essential to the foundation of the General Electric Building[64], the skyscraper that would become the centrepiece of the Rockefeller Center. Therefore – at least in the minds of the authors of the project – it served as a symbol of the resilience of a whole nation ready to reinstate itself as a "world pillar", a role the Great Depression had so violently undermined.

Examining the photograph more closely, however, one notices that this strategy of glorifying American pride and power fails in its intent, because the underlying heroic narrative is inconsistent with what the image actually *shows*. Behind the workers, in the background, we can see the city of New York and Central Park in the distance, fading in the mist. But the relation between the foreground and the background can be read and interpreted – that is, *framed* – in two different ways, corresponding to two opposite perspectives.

Moving from foreground to background, we realise that the focus is on the workers as the builders of the city centre, the creators – if only in a material sense – of New York's revival. This is the most immediate and common reading, which supports an *inclusive* perspective in which city and workers are in tune, as if parts of a single and coherent political whole (according to the Greek meaning of *polis*, which refers as much to the 'city' as to the 'sociocultural community').

However, if we move from background to foreground, this immense city with no perceivable borders seems to swallow the workers so that the distance between men and buildings turns into a vertiginous abyss. In this second way of interpreting – that is, of *framing* – the picture, the workers stand out from the background as if they were foreign to it: they are building something that will never belong to them. This dichotomy between makers and made, builders and built, leads to an *exclusive* perspective in which barriers

64 Originally known as the Radio Corporation of American Building, the GE Building was renamed the Comcast Building in 2016.

and social discrimination become manifest. All in all, nothing is farther from the utopian message conveyed by the photograph than the workers portrayed in it, who are completely cast adrift from the rich socio-economic fabric of downtown New York. They are misplaced, both literally and figuratively. Feet dangling in the void, they sit hundreds of metres above the ground without any protection, a metaphor for the precarious living without a safety net during the Great Depression. The most dangerous lunch break in the world was supposed to symbolise a nation unafraid to take risks and always intent on forging ahead because "anything is possible". However, it ended up showing precisely the opposite, portraying the working and living conditions of those who are, by definition, excluded from a social space that remains inaccessible to them.

At any rate, we should not forget that the message *Lunch Atop a Skyscraper* was meant to convey was at odds with the reality of life in 1932. After all, the financial crisis had yet to be reversed and there was little confidence in the ability of capitalism to rise from its ashes. Indeed, the first skyscrapers of the Rockefeller Center were the only ones to be built in the heart of Manhattan during those years. Its creator John D. Rockefeller Jr. presented himself as a mentor and benefactor who gave work to the masses and helped them improve their living conditions – a promoter of economic and social progress. Trying to convey a positive image of a tragic reality, *Lunch Atop a Skyscraper* perfectly embodied a liberal political ideology that would find its best expression a year later in Roosevelt's New Deal. The photograph is therefore the perfect counterpart to the emblematic skyscraper, the symbol of New York's vertical growth. Both the building and the picture are aimed at glorifying the positive, irenic, and triumphant "American spirit", a term the Dutch architect Rem Koolhaas significantly renamed 'Manhattanism'[65].

Thus, in its apparent simplicity or even naivety, *Lunch Atop a Skyscraper* is both mythifying and mystifying, as it represents a dramatic socio-economic situation in a favourable light, making it seem much less complex than it actually was. In an interview for *The Wall Street Journal*, historian Ken Johnston, director of the Historical and Fine Art Images section of the Corbis Agency (which

65 Rem Koolhaas, *Delirious New York: A Retroactive Manifesto for Manhattan* (New York: Oxford University Press, 1978).

holds the rights to the image), recalled: 'This is the first two years of the Great Depression. Usually when you saw lines of men, at that time, they'd be in a bread line, at a soup kitchen, not working and eating lunch'[66]. But from this gloomy statement he then drew the oddly optimistic conclusion that *Lunch Atop a Skyscraper* displays 'the worker in America in the 30s, keeping going and building'. However, contrary to Johnston's statement, the photograph did not display, but rather *staged* its content. It expressed something that failed to match reality, since its celebration of capitalism and the American way of life coincided at a time in which the fragile and eminently ideological nature of these constructs was being tragically exposed. At its inauguration, half of Rockefeller Center's offices were empty due to lack of tenants.

From the perspective of visual culture studies, it must be emphasised that photography, a medium associated with transparency and 'noninterventionist objectivity'[67], here turns out to be both opaque and strongly ambiguous, even more so if we consider that *Lunch Atop a Skyscraper* – as many studies have shown over time – is all but an "innocent" snapshot: on the contrary, it was orchestrated for purposes of advertising and propaganda. Yet, although the photograph was staged, the men on the skyscraper were not actors: they were actual construction workers at the Rockefeller Center, who really broke their backs and risked their lives every single day. A commemorative video broadcast by *Time Magazine* shows them at work, crossing over the metal beams like tightrope walkers, facing the void with no protection or safety net. Considering that these anonymous workers were mostly immigrants who came to New York in the early twentieth century[68], *Lunch Atop a Skyscraper* appears to symbolise the United States not as a land of equal opportunity,

66 Ken Johnston interviewed by Jackie Bischof for The Wall Street Journal, 20 September 2012.

67 Lorraine Daston and Peter Galison, *Objectivity* (New York: Zone Books, 2007), p. 123 and p. 187.

68 In *Men at Lunch*, an interesting documentary presented at the 2013 Toronto International Film Festival, Irish filmmakers Seán and Eamonn Ó Cualáin attempted to reconstruct the story behind *Lunch Atop a Skyscraper*, finally succeeding in identifying some of the workers with a reasonable degree of accuracy.

but as a place of inequality, non-integration, and exploitation. The America symbolised by the Rockefeller Center was built not only with the help of these workers, but also at the cost of their lives. As the so-called Sky Boys, men who faced death on a daily basis due to their work, remarked: 'We do not die, we are killed'[69].

There are actually several versions of the same subject, taken from different angles, and two other shots have recently been discovered: one showing the same eleven workers looking directly at the camera and waving at the photographer; the other showing four of them pretending to take a nap. We can reasonably conclude, then, that there was certainly more than one photographer on site[70]. However, the identity of the author of *Lunch Atop a Skyscraper* has also been questioned. After considering Charles Clyde Ebbets (presumably present at the Rockefeller Center), and then Lewis Hyne (who started his career photographing Ellis Island immigrants), in 2012 Corbis Images felt obliged to declare that the photograph should be considered an anonymous work until proved otherwise.

All these elements seem crucial both from a historical and from a theoretical point of view, as they force us to question not only the truth-value of this particular photograph, but also that which continues to be attributed to the photographic medium in general, even after numerous studies in the field of the history and theory of photography have demonstrated that there is no such thing as an image 'uncontaminated by interpretation'[71], nor can there ever be. Strictly speaking, as mentioned, it should be said that the

---

69 Alice Sparberg Alexiou, *The Flatiron: The New York Landmark and the Incomparable City That Arose with It* (New York: St. Martin's Griffin, 2010), p. 94.

70 All the more so because we know that the image of the four "sleeping" workers comes from the International News Photo archives, a photographic agency competing with Acme Newspictures, which owned the rights to Ebbets' original shot.

71 Lorraine Daston and Peter Galison, *Objectivity*, p. 139. On the nature of "realism" and the relationship between transparency and opacity in relation to the photographic medium, see in particular Kendall Walton, 'Transparent Pictures: On the Nature of Photographic Realism', *Critical Inquiry*, 11, 2 (1984), 246–77, as well as the criticism of this position expressed by Jean Lauzon in *La photographie malgré l'image* (Ottawa: Presses de l'Université d'Ottawa, 2002), pp. 30–34.

scene was not really *captured* but rather *constructed*: *Lunch Atop a Skyscraper* is a *mise-en-scène* rather than an objective, tangible proof documenting and celebrating the American attempt to make a socio-economic recovery from the Great Depression.

Now let us fast-forward about sixty years. In 1989, Duane Hanson presented a sculpture whose title – *Lunch Break* – and overall idea clearly allude to *Lunch Atop a Skyscraper*. However, Hanson's work is not merely a reformulation, but rather a 'remediation'[72] of the famous photograph, made three-dimensional through a different medium. And this remediation leads to a reframing of the original picture as well.

Compared to the serenity and confidence in the future that shone through *Lunch Atop a Skyscraper*, *Lunch Break* conveys a completely different atmosphere that immediately suggests moral confusion, social disintegration and loss of human dignity. Unlike their predecessors, relaxing together in a spirit of collaboration and mutual support, the three protagonists of the poor (and sad) meal staged by Hanson stare blankly in mute isolation from each other, immersed in their own thoughts. Instead of resting before going back to work, they are idle, as if paralysed, deadened by a pointless wait for something – hard to say what – that will never come.

These 'effigies of exhaustion', as Bruce Bégout puts it, show 'a double stillness'. The rigidity of their poses accentuates the intrinsic immobility of sculpture. Although the characters are supposedly represented 'during a break, a moment of rest between two activities'[73], their static poses clearly offer a form of social criticism:

> The break taken by the characters refers to a kind of weariness linked to activity itself. This is not the kind of rest that follows toil, but the abrupt interruption of work, like the symbol of sudden exhaustion. [...] Hanson's characters are really *idle*, they have nothing to do, to say, to think, no work to pursue, no immediate

---

72 In the sense given to the term by Jay David Bolter and Richard Grusin, *Remediation: Understanding New Media*, (Cambridge MA–London: The MIT Press, 1999).

73 Bruce Bégout, 'Duane Hanson grandeur nature', in *Duane Hanson. Le Rêve américain*... (Paris: Actes Sud–Parc de la Villette, 2010), pp. 7–12 (p. 11).

> or distant goal. They stagnate in the absence of a project, whether at work or not. They call to mind Anders' 'worldless people'. These unemployed, precarious workers, vulnerable and unsuited to the world of overproduction and profitability, unwittingly suspend their relationship with the world and society, and live their life as a 'being there' without a horizon.[74]

The signs of homologation and conformism are everywhere: a Fila t-shirt stretched on a beer belly, the empty Domino's takeaway pizza box, a couple of Coca-Cola cans and the inevitable pack of red Marlboro peeping out of the pocket of a pair of blue jeans. What is missing is any sign whatsoever of interest in the present or confidence in the future. These workers are as incapable of construction as they are of dreaming: 'A perfect embodiment of the banality of the contemporary American way of life, they seem like specimens of a culture of the end of the twentieth century exhibited in a twenty-first century museum of civilization'[75]. Compared to *Lunch Atop a Skyscraper*, *Lunch Break* creates an astonishing semantic inversion: the American dream, as epitomised by the famous photograph, turned into a nightmare.

The radical change in the meaning of the image is not only determined by the change of epoch and historical context, but also by the use of different media. Due to the distance that every photograph establishes between itself and the observer, *Lunch Atop a Skyscraper* projected the workers into an ideal and mythical dimension. On the contrary, *Lunch Break* takes advantage of the "fleshiness" of sculpture to bring them back – both literally and metaphorically – down to earth. Instead of the girder hanging at a vertiginous height, we are given a far more prosaic scaffolding, placed at ground level and therefore ultimately devoid of utility and meaning. The former symbol of the glorious American renaissance has now become an icon of disillusionment and social malaise.

Ultimately, what is at stake is the truth-value attributed to the two media. *Lunch Atop a Skyscraper* showed that photography, generally regarded as *the* medium of mechanical fidelity to reality, can in fact operate as an elaborate staging. On the contrary,

---

74 *Ibid.*, pp. 11–12.
75 John K. Grande, 'Americanacirema', *Espace : Art actuel*, 28 (1994), 19–22 (p. 21).

Hanson's hyperrealistic sculpture, which, upon first inspection, seems particularly misleading because of its illusionism, which links it to the age-old tradition of *trompe-l'œil*, turns out to be far more adherent to reality than its model. By showing the unglamorous end of the American dream, it allows us to unveil the mystification of reality produced by the original photograph and to see everything that this dream has actually brought with it, namely the tragic condition and alienation of way too many people.

But how is it that this sculpture, which, from a purely physical point of view, is *identical* to the deceiving mannequins at Madame Tussauds and Grévin, manages to achieve the privileged status of a work of art? How can it turn illusion and deception into a particular form of truth, thus escaping the ordinary fate of the hyperrealistic figures commonly associated with mere trickery and deception because of their giving 'an appearance of life that is not life, an appearance of reality that is not reality'[76]?

Reiterated countless times over the centuries, the criticism of hyperrealism as a legitimate art form is based on the principle that so-called "high" art must go beyond merely replicating reality or deceiving the observer. The emblematic example of ordinary wax figures makes it easy to understand why they have been so often banned from the aesthetic domain. They are not considered works of art because any activity solely aimed at the servile reproduction of reality is doomed to generate objects that, while perhaps appearing curious or even pleasant, are inevitably devoid of the originality, uniqueness, and truth which are characteristic of the artist's genius. Whether they are directly cast from life (as is most often the case in Hanson's work) or not, hyperrealistic sculptures are immediately associated with mechanical processes that seem to invalidate *a priori* any aesthetic claim. The detractors of hyperrealism tirelessly refer to the paradigmatic criticism formulated by Diderot in the eighteenth century: 'I have been told about a sculptors' trick. Do you know what they do? They take plaster moulds of a model's feet, hands, and shoulders. By filling these moulds, casts are made that they subsequently use in their compositions just as they are. To be sure, this is an easy way to

76 Jules-François-Félix Husson, also known as Champfleury, *Les excentriques* (Paris: Michel Lévy Frères, 1855), p. 307.

approach the truth of nature; yet it must no longer be regarded as the merit of a skilful sculptor, but rather of an ordinary smelter'[77].

Roughly thirty years after Diderot in 1790, Immanuel Kant made a similar statement, which is contained in the 45th paragraph of his *Critique of Judgement* entitled 'Fine art is an art, so far as it has at the same time the appearance of being nature'. Indeed, we might reasonably confuse the title as a plea for hyperrealism. But Kant clarifies that what he is in fact claiming is that art should look like nature, but only to an extent: 'Art can only be termed beautiful where we are conscious of its being art, while yet it has the appearance of nature. We must be able to look upon fine art as nature, although we recognize it to be art'[78]. Here, too, the emphasis is that viewers must be able to immediately recognise the picture *as a picture*. In other words, they must be fully aware of the iconic nature of what they are looking at. An overly precise imitation of nature is ultimately detrimental to the work of art, preventing it from expressing any form of truth.

So what should we think of *Lunch Break*, a work that instead seems to testify *in favour* of a mimesis pushed to the extreme? In order to avoid this apparent contradiction, we might claim that all hyperrealist mannequins, while striking the observer for their illusionistic power, do not succeed in completely deceiving. These works clearly reveal their iconic nature, and it is for this reason that they have been able to overcome controversies and even find their place in fine art museums.

Yet there is a specific moment in the history of art when this argumentative strategy permanently lost its validity: the moment when imitation managed to leave no gap, no difference between the image and its referent. In 1964, at the Stable Gallery in New York, Andy Warhol presented his replicas of packaging boxes stamped with Brillo, Kellogg's, Campbell's and Del Monte logos. Insofar as these sculptures reproduce original boxes down to the smallest detail, they are often confused with ready-mades. This is certainly a mistake, but a very significant one, because it stems from a mimetic fidelity taken to such extremes that any distinction

77 Denis Diderot, *Salon 1763*, ed. by Jean Seznec and Jean Adhémar, 4 vols (Oxford: Clarendon Press, 1975), I, pp. 247–48.

78 Kant, *Critique of Judgment*, p. 135.

between originals and copies fades away. Likeness turns into identity by virtue of the 'invasion [...] of real life within imaginary universes'[79] that has characterised many twentieth-century artistic currents. In the eyes of the observer, nothing except location differentiates the work of art from its model. However, it is precisely this difference in location that poses a problem: it is unclear why one of these boxes should adorn the temple of consumerism (the supermarket), while the other the temple of aesthetic enjoyment (the museum). Tracing this problem back to Duchamp and his famous *Fountain* would not be very helpful, since that urinal was a real urinal, and not the *imitation* of a urinal. Warhol does not simply choose an ordinary object and call it art, but rather carefully imitates an ordinary object to the point of making it a work of art *precisely by virtue of this hyper-mimetic act*.

Taking the example of the Brillo Box, we cannot ignore just how ordinary the reproduced object actually is. Although its design is undoubtedly highly refined (its creator James Harvey, himself an artist, was inspired by the abstract art of the time), the Brillo Box is still a simple soap pad container; nothing more than a common everyday object. Now, these two characteristics – the striking resemblance to the model and the rather ordinary character of the model itself – are precisely the same as those that feature in *Lunch Break*[80].

With regard to the first aspect – adherence to reality – the extreme attention to detail, as well as the use of real hair and all kinds of accessories, allowed Hanson to achieve such an extreme degree of realism that it becomes almost impossible to determine at first sight whether the figures are images or workers in the flesh. As for the second point – the triviality of the subject represented – it is worth noting that Hanson dedicated most of

79 Steinmetz, *L'esthétique phénoménologique de Husserl*, p. 131. Steinmetz rightly emphasizes all the difficulties that Husserlian phenomenology encounters when confronted not only with contemporary hyperrealism, but also with so-called abstract art.

80 It is therefore no coincidence that Hanson paid homage to Warhol by placing a Brillo box on the wheeled rubbish bin of his *Queenie*, the black office cleaner protagonist of one of his 'sculptures of life' – an expression that can be understood either as 'representations of the living' or as 'representations taken from life', as they were actually made using plaster casts.

his career to documenting the lives of those nameless, ordinary men and women we pass by daily on the street without ever really seeing them:

> People are Duane Hanson's main subject. His art-people are the medium of his message. They are very specific people. They are not special characters, and not at all conspicuous, since they come from the masses. All his life Duane Hanson noticed them, and his trained eye often picked them out on the edge of the crowd, because even the masses left these people no room in their centers – mentally or physically.[81]

In contrast to Madame Tussauds' wax figures, which are rightly discredited from an aesthetic point of view, it is evident that *Lunch Break* does not take fidelity to reality as a goal in itself. By reversing the traditional argument that hyperrealism cannot be regarded as a genuine art form, Hanson shows that an exaggerated, even hyperbolic, resemblance to reality is indeed capable of drawing attention to elements that are all too often neglected, both in reality itself and in its artistic representation. And these are the exact elements that *Lunch Atop a Skyscraper* sought to conceal. In *Lunch Break*, the overlap between reality and fiction is not aimed at merely deceiving the viewer, but at arousing a broader reflection on the value of human existence in American capitalist society and in the cultural model that it embodies.

From this perspective, we can better understand why the artist considered all criticisms that attempted to reduce his work to a simple replica of reality as unfair and unjustified: 'I'm not duplicating life, I'm making a statement about human values. I show the empty-headedness, the fatigue, the aging, the frustration. These people can't keep up with the competition. They're left out, psychologically handicapped'[82]. Hanson made sure that the last

81 Thomas Buchsteiner, 'Art Is Life, and Life Is Realistic', in *Duane Hanson: More than Reality*, ed. by Thomas Buchsteiner and Otto Letze (Ostfildern: Hatje Cantz, 2007), pp. 68–79 (p. 69).

82 Duane Hanson quoted in Martin H. Bush (ed.), *Sculptures by Duane Hanson* (Wichita: Wichita State University, 1985), p. 15. The only criticism against Duane Hanson's work that I deem relevant (although not entirely acceptable) was brought forward by J.J. Charlesworth in an article significantly entitled 'Is Duane Hanson's Sentimentality for

would be first and the forgotten would be placed centre stage, at least for the duration of a museum visit; his *Sculptures of the American Dream* (as a retrospective exhibition dedicated to him was ironically and at the same time quite appropriately titled) has allowed us to see – one might be tempted to say, to *really* see – 'these losers in life and heroes of everyday life'[83]. People like Roy or, indeed, the workers of *Lunch Break*.

By trying to subvert *Lunch Atop a Skyscraper*'s mythical dimension and to show the tragic reality of everyday life, Hanson did everything he could to nullify the distance between image and prototype. If the photographic medium, by its very nature, entails an insurmountable gap between the representing image and the represented object, which makes its products immediately identifiable as pictures, sculpture gives its *sujets* an astonishing effect of presence. A statue (especially a hyperrealistic statue)

Working People Noble or Just Patronizing?' (Artnet News, 9 June 2015). Charlesworth claims that the American artist, by voluntarily ignoring the 'cosmopolitan, metropolitan world of people who spend their time going to art galleries – the trendy, the aspirational, the well-off', failed to consider that his sculptures, once exhibited in public galleries – places not generally frequented by the individuals represented in Hanson's work – would in fact be at the mercy of the very audience he had chosen to disregard. By refusing to take into account the social context in which his works would be exhibited, Hanson was not able to foresee that the public, instead of sympathising with the ordinary folk that make up the contemporary American working class, would actually look down on them with an air of condescension or even indifference.

83 Buchsteiner, 'Art Is Life, and Life Is Realistic', p. 69. In 2006, the Mexican artist Dulce Pinzón realised a work conceptually similar to Duane Hanson's: a series of nineteen colour photographs entitled *The Real Story of the Superheroes*, representing Latin-American immigrants in the workplace dressed as famous superheroes. The paradoxical juxtaposition of contradictory elements – the ordinary individual and the superhero, the banal tasks and the fantastic costumes, the servile and the domineering – alerts the observer to the visual metaphor being proposed: just as superheroes clothe their real, modest identities, the supremacy of the economic and socio-cultural model represented by the United States masks the fact that this system only thrives on the misery of "others", the anonymous men and women working under unfavourable conditions for miserable wages. By transforming a pizza delivery-man into Superman, Pinzón seeks to 're-educate our gaze with satire so that it can grasp this new urban epic'; Sylvie Kande, 'Note de lecture', *Autrepart. Revue de sciences sociales au Sud*, 67–68 (2013), 281–83 (p. 282).

shares our same space and time – we could say that it breathes the same air as us. In addition, although it is made to be seen, a sculpture always implies a particularly marked haptic and motor stimulation: contemplation from a distance gives way to "face-to-face" experience and to the desire to touch, caress, and walk around the image. This fleshy dimension of sculpture can be further enhanced by polychromy and the use of special materials such as fiberglass or polyester resins, which, unlike marble or bronze, dramatically increase the proximity between the observer and the artwork[84].

Hanson, however, had to deal with an apparently insuperable obstacle characteristic of the medium of sculpture. Despite their surprising realism and although cast from life, Roy and the three workers depicted in *Lunch Break* cannot ultimately deceive the viewer, primarily because they do not move. Even if they share our space, we can (mis)take them for real human beings only for a few moments. Thus, despite all the artist's efforts, the distance between image and reality is not entirely deleted. Yet even the absence of movement (which can be regarded as the ultimate frame of hyperrealistic sculptures, for it re-establishes a distance between the world of the image and the real world) has recently been challenged by a new reframing of the image, which is paradoxically based on a return to the photographic medium.

In 2003, American visual artist Sharon Lockhart took photographs of Hanson's work being installed at Edinburgh's Scottish National Gallery of Modern Art. *Lunch Break Installation* consists of four photographs, one taken shortly after the other. The mechanical eye captured not only Hanson's likenesses, but also the real workers setting up the installation. Looking at each image independently, it is almost impossible to distinguish the flesh-and-blood installers from the polyvinyl mannequins because the photographic medium, by definition, excludes movement, thereby eliminating the decisive

84 In examining the exemplary case of busts, Ernst Gombrich pointed out that different materials have a very different impact on the observer. When facing a marble bust, 'we do not, as a rule, take it to be a representation of a cut-off head'; a wax bust, on the contrary, 'often causes us uneasiness because it oversteps the boundary of symbolism'; Gombrich, *Art and Illusion*, p. 60.

– though not the only – element by which the observer of Hanson's sculptures can distinguish fiction from reality.

Precedents to Lockhart's experiment can be found in Karl Schenker's doll figures from the 1920s and, more recently, in Hiroshi Sugimoto's artworks. By taking a black and white picture of fully clothed wax figures, both artists offered a reflection on the ambiguity and permeability of the borders between images and their referents. When looking at their shots, it is extremely hard to decide whether they show real bodies or wax models, for in both cases black and white photography establishes the very same distance between body and image. In Schenker's case, in particular, the dolls were created and dressed by the artist himself, attaining such a level of perfection and verisimilitude that it is almost impossible to distinguish them from real people. No surprise, then, that the editors of *Die Dame* – the magazine Schenker worked for – decided to give his series of photographs the provocative title: 'Fashion models or wax figures?'[85]

Unlike her predecessors, though, Lockhart gives viewers one last chance to discriminate between the realm of reality and that of fiction, as she presents four photographs instead of one. Moving from one image to another, we finally realise that two of the workers change their position, whereas the others – that is to say, Hanson's sculptures – remain perfectly still. But this "spot-the-difference" game is complicated by the fact that the four photographs were not taken from the same angle, each of them being rotated 90 degrees compared to the previous one. This gives the impression that the mannequins also move, even though what changes is only the angle, that is, the framing.

Thus, one of the crucial elements of Lockhart's work is the time and effort it takes to correctly discern what is being presented. By forcing the observer to actively search for elements that distinguish mannequins from real workers, the artist invites us to reflect on the essentially artificial (and therefore manipulative) character of *all* images – including Hanson's installation. If *Lunch Break* denounced the mystification underlying *Lunch Atop a Skyscraper*, *Lunch Break Installation* shows in turn that even Hanson's work,

85 On this, see Miriam Halwani (ed.), *Karl Schenker's Mondäne Bildwelten* (Köln: König, 2016).

despite its hyperbolic realism and mechanical adherence to reality, cannot escape the fate of all images, which are doomed not to duplicate the real but to give it a form – and thus an interpretation – that is inevitably particular, subjective, and biased. Lockhart's photo series is a work of art not only about another work of art (Hanson's) but also about itself and about art as such. It is a meta-artistic take on the process of framing and reframing "reality" that is the *sine qua non* of all images.

This meta-artistic reflection also raises questions about the relation of photography to sculpture. If Hanson's installation risks being interpreted as a criticism of photography *tout court*, Lockhart's work implies, on the contrary, a valorisation of the photographic medium. Not only does her work differentiate between reality and fiction, between sculptures and people in the flesh, but also and above all it rehabilitates those "average men" to whom Hanson devoted his entire artistic work. After all, these are the men who set up the installation, making it available to the public. Hanson unravelled the mystifying epic underlying *Lunch Atop a Skyscraper* by showing the tragedy of lives without hope, without dreams, without a future. For this reason, he chose to present the subjects of his sculptures in static poses, as motionless as all sculptures necessarily are: 'In the world of infinite mobilisation of forces and talents', Hanson's individuals show 'a form of passive resistance by temporarily suspending their participation'[86]. The immobility of sculpture perfectly matches the existential immobility of the subjects portrayed.

For Lockhart, the very same question of immobility is framed differently. Her work, of course, is also subject to the immobility of the photographic medium, which plunges reality into a 'fixing bath'[87]. Forced to show her subjects in pictures, the artist risks reducing the flesh-and-blood workers to the same level as the polyvinyl figures, thus transmitting a message similar to Hanson's – namely, that the protagonists of the "American dream" are nothing but lifeless images of themselves. But that is precisely why Lockhart decided to take four photographs instead of one. In so doing, she shows the men *active* at work, whereas Hanson's figures remain tragically idle and *inactive*. It is therefore the photographic

86 Bégout, 'Duane Hanson grandeur nature', p. 12.
87 Philippe Dubois, *L'acte photographique* (Bruxelles: Labor, 1983), p. 163.

medium that allows Lockhart to convey a message that relativises, rebalances, and reframes Hanson's own "truth", which is itself, of course, a reframing of the "truth" of *Lunch Atop a Skyscraper*. But if we look more closely, there is yet another framing at play: the choice of the author of this book to propose (to *construct*) a path that leads from a 1930s photograph to its evolution in various contexts – contexts that, *precisely because of this framing*, also retrospectively shed new light on the "original" context.

4. *Immersive Environments*

May 1990. The forty-third edition of the Cannes Film Festival. Akira Kurosawa presents the world premiere of his controversial latest work: *Dreams*. The film consists of eight episodes that, as a sort of intellectual biography, narrate some significant stages of the Japanese director's life, charting his aspirations, fears, and obsessions. In the fifth segment, 'Crows', the actor Akira Terao plays a young artist – an alter ego of Kurosawa himself – visiting a museum and contemplating, in total solitude, some famous works by van Gogh. The first shot shows a self-portrait from 1889. The camera remains perfectly still, lingering for a few seconds on it. Suddenly, the protagonist literally enters the scene as if from behind us. Then the camera swiftly pans over more paintings: *The Starry Night*, a version of the *Sunflowers*, and *Wheatfield with Crows*. With a quick back-reveal, it follows Terao-Kurosawa as he sits down to contemplate the paintings from a distance. Soon after, the young man retrieves his tools of the trade (a box of colours, a couple of canvases and an easel) and gets up, ready to leave the room.

He passes by Van Gogh's *Chair*, *The Langlois Bridge*, and *Bedroom in Arles*, before stopping and returning to *The Langlois Bridge*. He puts on his hat and magically finds himself inside the painting, a few metres from the bridge. Thanks to a cinematic trick, what a moment (and a frame) ago was van Gogh's canvas turns into an animated landscape. The frame of the painting disappears, the silence is broken by Chopin's Prelude Op. 28, No. 15, and we spectators are projected into the image together with the protagonist, ready to follow him in search of the Dutch painter, impersonated by none other than Martin Scorsese (Fig. 7).

Fig. 7 – Two shots from *Dreams* by A. Kurosawa (1990)

The apprentice arrives to find some women washing clothes by the bridge. They inform him that van Gogh has just been discharged from the psychiatric hospital and is already looking around for new sources of inspiration. We start the search and finally find him, alone, painting frantically in the middle of a wheat field. Interrupted, but not at all surprised, by the arrival of Terao-Kurosawa, the master starts to speak: 'To me this scene is beyond belief. A scene that looks like a painting does not make a painting. But if you take the time and look closely, all the nature has its own beauty. And when that natural beauty is there, I just lose myself in it. And then, as if it's in a dream, the scene just paints itself for me'.

As if in Chinese boxes, this statement of poetics is not only valid for van Gogh who immerses himself in nature 'as if in a dream', but also for the young apprentice who plunges himself into van Gogh's work, passing from detached contemplation to an attitude where the typical distance of aesthetic enjoyment is progressively reduced to the point of vanishing completely. But the same also holds true for us, the spectators, who immerse ourselves in Kurosawa's filmic dream. Van Gogh's description of artistic activity

> happens to correspond to the phenomenological description of the standard film-viewing experience, namely, the disappearance into the 'nonthematic' both of real space (the movie theatre, the world, our seat, ourselves) and of the fictional topos, the (on-)screen. A painting is not hanging on the wall, a film is not on, or 'in' the screen – for there are no longer such things as 'a screen,' 'a wall.' The painting, the film, constitute their own self-consistent world (but nonthematic as such). Coleridge's suspension of disbelief is still a partial formula: what is really suspended is the very awareness of the difference between belief and disbelief, reality and fiction. What collapses, then, is the measurable spatial distance and distinction between the subject and the object. The moviegoer is no longer watching the film, nor is he co-present in it (the artifice Kurosawa was nonetheless constrained to use): he is rather 'in a state of film.' And he is *in* that space, rather than surrounded by it.[88]

Recall Simmel's anathema to any artistic experimentation that might offer 'a bridge through which, as it were, the world could get in or from which the picture could get out'[89]. Now, getting inside the image means breaking the frame of representation in the opposite

88 José Manuel Martins, '"Crows" vs "Avatar": or, 3D vs Total-Dimension Immersion', *Film and Media Studies*, 8 (2014), 79–96 (p. 91).
89 *Ibid.*, pp. 12–13.

direction to the one we have previously described. Husserl's wax lady and Hanson's hyperrealistic museum guard came out of the image-world to enter actual reality. Now it is the other way around. It is the spectator (of the painting, of the movie) who finds himself brought inside the frame. In this sense, Kurosawa's choice of precisely a bridge – among van Gogh's many paintings – to symbolise the crossing of the threshold between image and reality is anything but random. After all, the director's dream is only a chapter in the long history of the quest for immersion into iconic or "virtual" worlds – a history epitomized by the legend of Wu Tao-tsu, a Chinese painter of the T'ang dynasty who entered one of his own paintings only to disappear together with the Emperor Xuan Zong. This tale was retold by Marguerite Yourcenar in the oriental novel 'How Wang-Fô Was Saved'[90]. Here, another Chinese painter is accused of making the emperor believe, through his paintings, that the world is more beautiful than it actually is. Sentenced to death, he saves himself by completing one last work. All of a sudden, the painted sea waves acquire a real texture, overflow from the canvas and slowly invade the room before Wang-Fô departs by boat with his faithful assistant Ling, eventually disappearing inside the painting[91].

It is interesting to note that in Yourcenar's story the threshold between reality and representation is crossed in *both* directions. At first, the image-world exits the borders of the frame to invade the real world; then the real world penetrates the frame and merges with the image-world. But on closer inspection the same bi-directional movement also takes place in the case of hyperrealistic works placed outside the frame of ordinary exhibition spaces. This is for instance the case of Husserl's wax lady, as well as of some of Duane Hanson's sculptures, which are positioned in such a way as to make it difficult, if not impossible, to immediately recognise them as images. As we have seen, a hyperrealistic figure tends to

90 Marguerite Yourcenar, 'How Wang-Fô was Saved' (1936), in *Oriental Tales*, trans. by Alberto Manguel (New York: Farrar, Straus & Giroux, 1985), pp. 3–20.

91 For a careful reconstruction of the theme and an analysis of its repercussions on Western visual philosophy and culture, see Andrea Pinotti, 'The Painter through the Fourth Wall of China: Benjamin and the Threshold of the Image', in *Benjamin-Studien 3*, ed. by Sigrid Weigel and Daniel Weidner (Munich: Fink, 2014), pp. 133–49.

break the frame of representation and enter our own world. Yet if it succeeds in its intent, we also become part of its world, of the world of representation, unwittingly entering the iconic universe. The two directions (from inside the frame to outside and vice versa) are therefore not necessarily mutually exclusive, but can coexist or even coincide. Hegel noted this while meditating on the extraordinary presence-effect of certain works of art:

> If great portraits confront us through all the means at the disposal of art, in their full vitality, we already have in this *amplitude* of their existence this advance and emergence from their frames [*Hervortreten, Hinausschreiten aus ihrem Rahmen*]. For example, in Van Dyck's portraits, especially when the position of the sitter is not entirely *en face* but slightly turned away, the frame has looked to me like the door into the world that the sitter is entering [*hereintritt*].[92]

One particularly telling example illustrates this process of osmosis between reality and representation that occurs once the frame is breached: the *Sacri Monti*, a precursor to the illusory apparatuses of the diorama and panorama[93]. Originating in Northern Italy in the late fifteenth century and later spreading to other parts of Catholic Europe (as well as, in more recent times, to the United States and South America)[94], the Sacred Mountains consist of groups of "chapels" and other buildings

92 Georg Wilhelm Friedrich Hegel, *Aesthetics: Lectures on Fine Art*, trans. by Thomas Malcolm Knox, 2 vols (Oxford: Oxford University Press, 1975) II, p. 852.

93 On this, see Erkki Huhtamo, *Illusions in Motion: Media Archaeology of the Moving Panorama and Related Spectacles* (Cambridge MA–London: The MIT Press, 2013).

94 For an introductory comparative overview, see George Kubler, 'Sacred Mountains in Europe and America', in *Christianity and the Renaissance: Image and Religious Imagination in the Quattrocento*, ed. by Timothy G. Verdon and John Henderson (Syracuse: Syracuse University Press, 1990), pp. 413–41. On Sacred Mounts in the US, see: Hillary Kaell, *Walking Where Jesus Walked: American Christians and Holy Land Pilgrimage* (New York: New York University Press, 2014); Stephanie Stidham Rogers, *Inventing the Holy Land: American Protestant Pilgrimage to Palestine, 1865–1941* (Lanham: Lexington Books, 2011); Annabel Jane Wharton, *Selling Jerusalem: Relics, Replicas, Theme Parks* (Chicago: University of Chicago Press, 2006); Burke O. Long, *Imagining the Holy Land: Maps, Models, and Fantasy Travels* (Bloomington: Indiana University Press, 2003).

intended to evoke, in a natural setting, the most famous holy places (Bethlehem, Nazareth, Jerusalem, the sites of the Passion). Framed within such architectural structures, extremely realistic painted sceneries and lifelike statues – often provided with real hair, glass eyes, furniture and clothing – illustrate different religious subjects, ranging from the life and Passion of Christ to the life of the Virgin, of some saints, or to the Mysteries of the Rosary (Fig. 8).

Fig. 8 – *Sacro Monte* at Varallo, Chapel 27.
Giovanni d'Enrico and Tazio da Varallo, Jesus before Pilate (ca. 1615)

The cumulative spell of architecture, painted backgrounds, and hyperrealistic sculptures is what makes the *Sacri Monti* especially engaging. The visitors come to feel like they are part of a spectacle which has very little to do with a passive and detached *spectare*; progressing from chapel to chapel, they find themselves caught up in an affective relation with the subjects depicted, concretely *immersed* in an environment that makes use of every means to create the most vivid re-enactment of the main episodes of the Biblical narratives, and to minimize the distance between the beholders on the one side and the pictures on the other. Hyperrealism calls this separation between the iconic and the non-iconic into question: the reality of both the natural landscape and the architectonic setting blends with the "unreality" of the image-world, as fashioned by the lifelike sculptures and paintings, to the point that visiting, for instance, the Sacred Mountain of Varallo, feels like wandering not through a sanctuary in the province of Vercelli but through a veritable 'New Jerusalem', as Carlo Borromeo used to say.

In his ground-breaking book *The Power of Images*, which meditates on how beholders affectively respond to hyperrealistic pictures, David Freedberg focuses on the *Sacri Monti* and, more specifically, on the ambiguous role played by the grilles that keep the visitors separated from the scenes depicted inside the chapels. These barriers – together with frames, pedestals, showcases and so on – fall within the broader semantic category of the border, that is, of the 'artifice that, in a given space, designates an iconic or plastic statement as an organic unit'[95]. In the specific case of the *Sacri Monti*, the grille-border not only defines the space inside the chapels as an iconic space, but also the space outside as external, i.e. as belonging to the real world, to the world "in flesh and blood". Indeed, it is only by virtue of the border that external space 'is given its status of exteriority'[96].

Freedberg maintains that these barriers prevent the viewer from checking whether the figures are actually made of flesh, so that 'the suspension of final proof and the urge to verify makes the perception of the body as real still more acute'[97]. And again a few lines later:

95 Groupe μ, 'Sémiotique et rhétorique du cadre', p. 115.
96 *Ibid.*, p. 116.
97 David Freedberg, *The Power of Images: Studies in the History and Theory of Response* (Chicago: The University of Chicago Press, 1989), p. 196.

> Only the grille prevents the spectator from moving among these actors and from discoursing with them; but that interposition, that barrier, only serves to heighten the sense of realism. One cannot get in to prove that they are just stuffed or wooden figures; one must believe, and one does believe, that they are real, however much one may wonder at the kind of craftsmanship that makes the figures appear so vivid. They are beings like us, and we are like them.[98]

As sound and seemingly convincing as these remarks might seem, one should also stress that the *Sacro Monte* at Varallo, to which Freedberg here refers, underwent drastic alterations over the centuries. As pointed out by Alessandro Nova, not only were the elaborate grilles absent from the initial project, but they also came to denote 'a deliberate rejection of the purpose of the original structures, which pilgrims had been encouraged to enter and experience more directly'[99].

Similar arguments can be found in the official nomination proposal submitted in 2000 by the Italian Minister of Cultural Heritage and Activities for the inscription of the *Sacri Monti* of Piedmont and Lombardy on UNESCO's World Heritage List:

> In the 17th century, for obvious reasons of preservation, grilles and bars were added that only allow people to look at the sacred scenes from the outside, through windows opened specifically for this purpose on both sides of the chapels. Yet this was not how the whole setting was originally meant to look like, for the scenes were intended to be animated by pilgrims walking through them inside the chapels, thus becoming themselves part of the "great theatre of the mountains" that the *Sacri Monti* aimed to represent.[100]

98 *Ibid.*, pp. 197–198.

99 Alessandro Nova, 'Popular Art in Renaissance Italy: Early Response to the Holy Mountain at Varallo', in *Reframing the Renaissance: Visual Culture in Europe and Latin America, 1450–1650*, ed. by Claire J. Farago (New Haven–London: Yale University Press, 1995), pp. 113–26 (p. 121).

100 Italian Minister of Cultural Heritage and Activities, *Le paysage culturel des Monts-Sacrés du Piémont et de Lombardie: Proposition d'inscription de biens sur la liste du Patrimoine Mondial*, December 2000. The request was accepted in 2003.

On the one hand, one can therefore go along with Freedberg in saying that the grilles perceptually increase the sense of realism insofar as they prevent the visitors from getting too close to the simulacra. On the other, however, one should also acknowledge that these barriers, by keeping the pilgrims outside the chapels, draw a peculiar demarcation line that does not reduce, but rather significantly enhances distantiation. The interposed distance between the viewers and the pictures has three different and complementary functions. *Physically*, it obviously contributes to preserving the integrity of the site. *Metaphysically*, it enhances the transcendent quality of the sacred events depicted. Directly referring to the chapels of the *Sacro Monte* at Varallo, Paul Philippot correctly points out that the Church 'has always been cognizant of the metaphysical suggestions that lie in the partial concealment of the object of worship and has occasionally exploited them with a great deal of psychological expertise'[101]. From this perspective, the grilles aim at 'stimulating the perception of contemplating a sacred mystery'[102]. This, in turn, is inextricably linked to the third function of those barriers: *aesthetically*, they establish a threshold between the real world of the visitors and the "unreal" world of the pictures.

Indeed, the grilles contribute to delimiting the iconic space, but this delimitation is precisely what the *Sacri Monti* were designed to forgo. Originally, the pilgrims were asked to enter the chapels and walk among the figures, surrounded by the frescoes. Such a kinaesthetic experience proved perfectly adequate for enabling visitors to become physically and affectively immersed in the scenes depicted. Despite being the most apparent, sight was but one of the senses involved: at Varallo, the pilgrims were encouraged to touch the facsimile of the sepulchre of Christ or the replica of His footprint; while looking at the narratives, they were expected to recite the most famous prayers; and they were also encouraged to imagine the sounds that might have been heard by those who

101 Paul Philippot, 'Restoration from the Perspective of the Humanities', in *Historical and Philosophical Issues in the Conservation of Cultural Heritage*, ed. by Nicholas Stanley Price, Mansfield Kirby Talley, and Alessandra Melucco Vaccaro (Los Angeles: Getty Conservation Institute, 1996), pp. 216–29 (p. 225).

102 *Ibid.*

had been physically present at the time the depicted events took place. In a nutshell, 'the viewer of Varallo was not a spectator but an actor-participant'[103].

Because they strive for maximum verisimilitude, the *Sacri Monti* have often been compared to Madame Tussauds museums and other similar attractions. In his *Alps and Sanctuaries* (1881), Samuel Butler enthusiastically described the tremendous impact of all of those counterfeits on the visitors: 'Listen to the hushed "oh bel!" which falls from them as they peep through grating after grating; and the more tawdry a chapel is, the better as a general rule they are contented. They like them as our own people like Madame Tussaud's'[104]. Commenting on this passage, Freedberg agrees that 'the parallel with Madame Tussaud's is most apt', for in both cases the 'fusion of image and prototype'[105] that is typical of hyperrealistic representations forces the viewers to bracket disbelief and to forget (if only for a moment) that they are seeing nothing but pictures, acting instead as if those figures were persons in the flesh. Yet the visitors' comments, as reported by Butler, point in a different direction: that whispered 'oh bel! (how beautiful!)' is the trademark of aesthetic judgement, and, as such, typically denotes a distance between the viewers and the scenes depicted. As we have seen, aesthetic enjoyment requires contemplation, which, in turn, requires detachment, opposition, distance – which is precisely what the *Sacri Monti* were originally intended to negate.

In this respect, the analogy between the Sacred Mountains and Madame Tussauds is only partially valid, owing much to the introduction of the grilles that keep the reality of the life-world clearly separate from the "unreality" of the image-world. By dramatically altering the pilgrims' spatial, psychological, and affective experiences[106], the barriers made a decisive contribution to increasing the viewers' detachment from the scenes depicted and to raising their awareness that what they

103 Nova, *Popular Art in Renaissance Italy*, p. 123.
104 Samuel Butler, *Alps and Sanctuaries of Piedmont and the Canton Ticino* (London: Bogue, 1881), p. 326.
105 Freedberg, *The Power of Images*, p. 200.
106 See Ryan Gregg, 'The Sacro Monte of Varallo as a Physical Manifestation of the Spiritual Exercises', *Athanor*, 22 (2004), 49–55.

see are "nothing but pictures", however strong the sense of a living presence these very same pictures may undoubtedly convey. The immersive, multisensory experience characteristic of the original concept of the *Sacri Monti* gradually gave way to (merely) visual contemplation, thus accentuating the distance between the visitors and the subjects "on show" and bringing about a detachment that paves the way to aesthetic contemplation.

To prevent any possible misunderstanding, this is not to claim that Madame Tussauds or the Sacred Mount at Varallo in its current configuration are *deprived* of any affective power. Of course they are not, and one has every reason to agree with Freedberg that no matter how capable we are of aesthetically distancing ourselves from the scenes before us, we will continue to perceive living beings, animated like us, made 'of (apparently) the same breath, blood, and flesh'[107]. Yet we cannot deny that the affective charge of hyperrealistic figures tends to unavoidably fade away as soon as they are *framed* and *displayed* in a context that clearly reveals what they seek to conceal, namely their representational status. Framing hyperrealistic pictures leads to an anaesthetisation (if not annihilation) of their affective power. Designed to convey the impression of sharing our same real space-time continuum, our same life-world, these *environmental pictures*, as one might call them, revert to traditional, representational pictures as soon as they are placed in a context that isolates them, unmasking them as mere semblances. Framing what was originally intended to remain unframed amounts to radically altering the very nature of its affective potential.

In their original configuration, the *Sacri Monti* were among the proto-immersive environments whose prehistory is sometimes traced back to the painted caves of the Palaeolithic[108], and

107 Freedberg, *The Power of Images*, p. 200.

108 On the highly controversial "shamanic" theory in relation to cave paintings, according to which the divide between image and reality might have been challenged by the performance of enchantments and by induced trances, so as to produce an immersive environment for ritual actions, see: Walter Burkert, *Structure and History in Greek Mythology and Ritual* (Berkeley–Los Angeles–London: University of California Press, 1979), pp. 88–94; Jean Clottes and David Lewis-Williams, *Les*

whose history has subsequently unravelled over the centuries in many different forms: the entirely frescoed rooms of Pompeian villas, the vertiginous *trompe l'œils* of baroque vaults, *tableaux vivants*, or the panoramas, dioramas, wax museums and magic lanterns of the eighteenth- and nineteenth-century, to mention but a few[109]. More recently, this journey of proto-immersive environments has extended to include cinema. And it is certainly no coincidence that the dawn of cinema itself is marked by the breaking of the representational frame, with the famous *Arrival of a Train at La Ciotat* by the Lumière brothers in 1895. The film celebrates the extraordinary illusionistic power of a medium that seems to allow the projected images to "pierce the screen" and enter the space of actual reality. Even in this case, however, the movement that leads to breaking the frame of representation can be reversed. At the beginning of the 1950s, the invention of Cinerama – a system of shooting and projection designed to produce a large image on a curved screen capable of "covering" the entire radius of human peripheral vision – gave new life to the dream of penetrating the screen and entering the image. The slogans chosen to advertise the new frontiers of the cinematographic medium – "It puts you in the picture", "It plunges you into a startling new world" – explicitly insisted on its unparalleled immersive power (Fig. 9).

chamanes de la Préhistoire. Transe et magie dans les grottes ornées (Paris: Le Seuil, 1996). For a survey of the state-of-the-art see Sophie Archambault de Beaune, 'Chamanisme et préhistoire : Un feuilleton à épisodes', *L'Homme*, 147 (1998), 203–19; Florian Berrouet, 'La part du corps : chamanisme et écriture', *Communication & Langages*, 186, 4 (2015), 5–25; Matteo Meschiari, 'Sciamanesimo paleolitico europeo. Paradigmi ermeneutici e riesame fenomenologico dell'arte parietale franco-cantabrica', in *Le origini sciamaniche della cultura europea*, ed. by Francesco Benozzo (Alessandria: Edizioni dell'Orso, 2015), pp. 21–54.

109 See, among others, Stephan Oettermann, *Das Panorama: Die Geschichte eines Massenmediums* (Frankfurt a.M.: Syndikat, 1980); Vanessa R. Schwartz, *Spectacular Realities: Early Mass Culture in Fin-de-Siècle Paris* (Berkeley–Los Angeles–London: University of California Press, 1998); Oliver Grau, *Virtual Art: From Illusion to Immersion* (Cambridge MA–London: The MIT Press, 2003); Huhtamo, *Illusions in Motion*.

Fig. 9 – Advertisement for Cinerama.

Around the same time, but on the other side of the world, Sergei Eisenstein was laying plans for a 'stereoscopic cinema' that would be able, by virtue of its irresistible three-dimensional effect, to "'bridge the gap", to "throw a line" across the "abyss" dividing the spectator from the actor'[110]. Piercing the screen frame in both directions, the *stereokino* would have the ability to '"pull" the spectator – with unprecedented intensity – into what was once the plane of the screen, and to "precipitate" upon him – with equally devastating force – all that had previously remained splayed out upon its reflective surface'[111]. Of course, in retrospect, it can be said that the journey toward realising the dream of *stereokino* has taken much longer and has proved much more difficult than Eisenstein could have imagined, given that the history of its closest relative, 3D cinema, is characterised more by unfulfilled great expectations and sensational failures (including at the box office) than by successes. Over the decades, the aspiration to completely immerse the spectator has led to an attempt to explore more and more "dimensions". Much focus has been placed on optical illusionism through the use of special glasses, but gradually, 3D cinema has begun to integrate new multi-sensory effects such as those provided by Dolby Surround, seat motion, smell, wind and water droplets, the presence of real actors, the use of interactive and immersive devices – and who knows what the future holds in store?

What remains of the theoretical framework proposed by Eisenstein – what he himself called his 'dream'[112] – is mainly the idea that humankind has a 'very basic, innate tendency'[113], an 'inherent natural urge', a 'deep-seated need'[114], an innate, evolutionary 'tendency'[115] 'to "penetrate" the audience and to "pull" it into the action'[116]. Throughout history, this hypothesis, both fascinating and problematic, has taken hold in a series of narratives that are centred around not only an increasing overlap between the image-world and reality but also a decreasing

110 Sergei Eisenstein, 'On Stereocinema' (1947), trans. by Sergey Levchin, in *3D Cinema and Beyond*, ed. by Dan Adler, Janine Marchessault, and Sanja Obradovic (Bristol: Intellect, 2013), pp. 20–59, (p. 29).

111 *Ibid.*, p. 26. And a few lines above (p. 23): 'What we have become accustomed to seeing as an image on the screen suddenly "swallows" us up into unprecedented depths, beyond the plane of the screen, or "thrusts out" at us with unprecedented force'.

112 *Ibid.*, p. 29.

113 *Ibid.*, p. 39.

114 *Ibid.*, p. 26.

115 *Ibid.*, p. 29

116 *Ibid.*

awareness of the difference between the two. From Plato's myth of the cave, whose prisoners cannot distinguish the shadow images from the real bodies that cast them, to the legend of Narcissus drowning in his own reflected image; from Descartes's hypothesis of an evil genius deceiving the human mind by offering it a surrogate of reality completely identical to actual reality, to its numerous contemporary interpretations, such as Daniel Dennett's 1978 thought experiment, the 'brain in a vat'[117], which was subsequently taken up by Hilary Putnam[118] in 1981 and made famous by *The Matrix* in 1999; from Calderón de la Barca's play *Life is a Dream*, in which the waking state becomes indistinguishable from the oneiric world, to Christopher Nolan's film *Inception*; from the cyberpunk poetics of *Strange Days*, where other people's experiences are recorded through electronic devices that capture the memories and physical sensations of those who wear them ('I sell experiences', the protagonist says), to the futuristic universe of the HBO television series *Westworld*, a disturbing amusement park designed to allow wealthy visitors to live out their most perverse fantasies with hyperrealistic androids, spending a few days in a parallel world 'with unlimited possibilities' ('We sell complete immersion', as one of the park managers states). In these and innumerable other examples, in different forms and with different nuances, the keyword is 'immersion', a metaphor for total involvement and absorption[119] in which the user is less and less able to distinguish between the reality of the world of life and the unreality (which at this point, however, is almost as real) of the image.

In short, it seems humanity has dreamt Eisenstein's dream over and over again, from the dawn of civilisation to the present day. Still, it has always been *a dream*, variously embodied in

117 Daniel C. Dennett, 'Where am I?', in Douglas R. Hofstadter and Daniel C. Dennett, *The Mind's I: Fantasies and Reflections on Mind and Soul* (New York: Basic Books, 1981), pp. 217–29.

118 Hilary Putnam, 'Brains in a Vat', in *Reason, Truth and History* (Cambridge: Cambridge University Press, 1981), pp. 1–21.

119 For an insight discussion of the many different meanings that have been rather confusingly attributed to the word 'immersion' and its cognate terms see Gordon Calleja, *In-Game: From Immersion to Incorporation* (Cambridge MA–London: The MIT Press, 2011).

myths, legends, thought experiments, and science fiction stories. Yet the question is whether that 'always' will ever be replaced with 'hitherto', that is, whether the most recent technological advances will make the dream of total immersion come true. Let us briefly follow the evolution of the three cases referred to earlier. The first, the Platonic cave, has found its contemporary heir in CAVE (a recursive acronym for Cave Automatic Virtual Environment); a room whose walls, covered by 360-degree, high-resolution, frameless screens generate three-dimensional images that completely surround the user. We might consider the second case the hi-tech updates of the iconic 3D cinema glasses: virtual reality headsets such as Oculus and Vive that offer the wearer an unprecedented immersive experience.

Our last example brings us back to where we started. Currently touring the world with enormous success and under various names (*Van Gogh Alive*; *Van Gogh: The Immersive Experience*; *Van Gogh: Multimedia Experience*) is an immersive van Gogh exhibition inaugurated in 2017. What distinguishes it from the countless others dedicated to the Dutch master is that it features none of his paintings. The artworks and their traditional frames are replaced by an innovative system of video projections and interactive installations that take up the whole interior of the host building. The result is an immersive environment that reproduces van Gogh's works on a far greater scale than the originals. Thus, the spectator has the impression of walking among the "paintings" before, in the last section of the exhibition, actually ending up *inside* them. Through the use of dedicated viewers and earphones, the visitor's role changes from that of an observer placed *in front of* images isolated from the real world through a frame to that of an experiencer placed *within* a virtual reality offering multisensory and kinaesthetic stimulations, as well as levels of interaction comparable to those of reality in the flesh (Fig. 10).

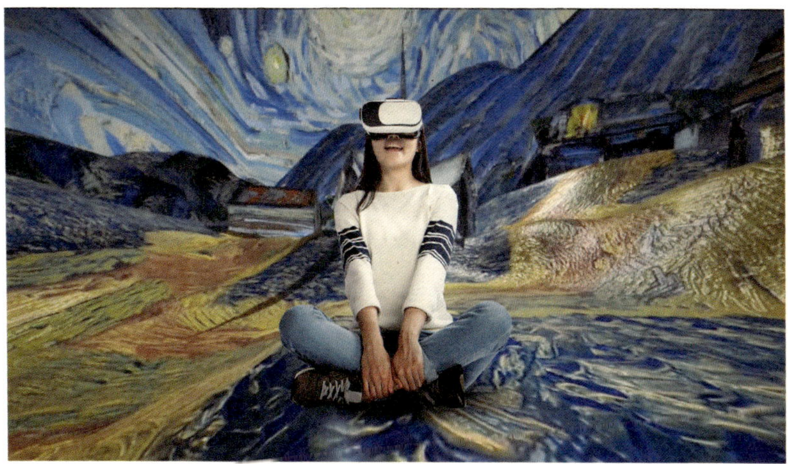

Fig. 10 – *Inside Painters: Van Gogh*
(project realised by Oniride under the patronage of the Van Gogh Museum)

One cannot help thinking whether Kurosawa would have liked this new kind of image experience. One thing is certain though: his dream – of crossing the threshold of the image-world to penetrate inside it – is being made increasingly real. But the road that leads to its complete fulfilment necessarily involves eliminating the frame as a fundamental element of the dispositif of representation: to quote Peter Sloterdijk, 'immersion as a method unframes [*Entrahmungsverfahren*] images and vistas, dissolving the boundaries with their environment'[120]. It is no coincidence that for some time now terms like 'borderless' and 'frameless' have become more and more popular, to the point that they currently represent an almost essential feature of the latest technological gadgets. Big corporations are competing to produce 'frameless displays'[121] and

120 Peter Sloterdijk, 'Architecture as an Art of Immersion' (2006), trans. by Anna-Christina Engels-Schwarzpaul, *Interstices*, 12 (2011), 105–09 (p. 105).

121 See Claudio Pinhanez, Mark Podlaseck, 'To Frame or Not to Frame: The Role and Design of Frameless Displays in Ubiquitous Applications', in *Ubiquitous Computing. Lecture Notes in Computer Science*, vol. 3660, ed. by Michael Beigl *et al.* (Berlin–Heidelberg: Springer, 2005). https://doi.org/10.1007/11551201_20.

full-screen mobile phones and televisions by moving or removing anything that can hamper the elimination of the frame, be it the camera, the fingerprint reader, or the home button.

A leader in this global trend, Samsung can now boast the highly immersive quality of its 'Infinity Display': no more edges, no more frames, just the screen to cover the whole surface of the device. Being deprived of (or rather freed from) all surrounding and isolating borders, the image displayed further increases the confusion between what is real and what is not, making the one indistinguishable from the other. Even in its advertisements, the South Korean company has long focused on promoting the immersivity of its devices. Consider, for instance, its TV that can reproduce a flower in such a detailed and realistic way that it can attract a hummingbird (a modern version of Pliny's narrative of the famous contest between Zeuxis and Parrhasius), or its virtual reality headset that can teach an ostrich to fly. The leading example, though, is the campaign launch of the Galaxy Note 8: the image returned by its phone screen is superimposed on the "real" landscape visible beyond the frame (now reduced to a minimum) to such an extent that it ends up replacing it. Additionally, through the use of a digital pen, which effectively "remediates" the allegedly obsolete painter's brush, the user is able to not only reproduce reality or make aspects of it visible that would otherwise remain invisible, but even to "overwrite" reality itself by – literally – designing a new one (Fig. 11).

Fig. 11 – Advertisement for the Samsung Galaxy Note 8 (2017)

And yet, in spite of the enormous progress made in recent decades in the field of augmented reality and virtual environments, one last obstacle continues to prevent us from achieving the ultimate immersive experience. This obstacle, which is itself a sort of frame, is the experiencer's *awareness* of not really being in another world, of being able to voluntarily stop playing the "image-game" at any time. Turning on a television or mobile phone, walking into a cinema to watch a movie in Cinerama format, wearing a headset that transports the viewer into a virtual reality online video game: all of these gestures and all of these technical devices are ultimately frames of representation and, as such, contribute to keeping a distance (though less and less noticeable) between the reality of the life-world and the unreality (though less and less unreal) of the image-world.

If total immersion arises 'when the artwork and technical apparatus, the message and medium of perception, converge into an inseparable whole'; if, 'at this point of calculated "totalisation", the artwork, which is perceived as an autonomous aesthetic object, can disappear as such for a limited period of time'; and if this is the point 'where being conscious of the illusion turns into unconsciousness of it'[122], then the goal is undoubtedly still far away. However, science fiction boasts an impressive track record of imagining futuristic scenarios in which the awareness (however residual it may be) of the necessarily mediated nature of any virtual and/or immersive experience is finally negated. This cannot be achieved by eliminating the medium, which is obviously impossible, but rather by linking it directly to human neural networks. The cyberpunk theme of using brain-computer interface (BCI) to generate *perceptions without the mediation of perceptive organs* anticipated the contemporary rush toward more and more sophisticated virtual reality brain implants that promise to realise the dream of 'neuroreality'[123], eventually fulfilling Peter Weibel's prophecy that, instead of *trompe l'œil*,

122 Grau, *Virtual Art*, pp. 348–49.

123 Kristin Houser, 'Neuroreality: The New Reality Is Coming. And It's a Brain Computer Interface', *Futurism*, 26 July 2017 (https://futurism.com/neuroreality-the-new-reality-is-coming-and-its-a-brain-computer-interface).

the next step in the increasingly immersive environmentalisation of the image experience might be *trompe le cerveau*[124].

Of course, one is free to disbelieve such prophecies and exercise some healthy scepticism[125]. And yet, given the latest technological developments, one cannot help but recall Louis Marin's view, namely that a frame is a mechanism that every representation includes in order to present itself in its function, its functioning, and its functionality *qua* representation: 'The more the transitive dimension presses its claims powerfully, the more "mimetic" transparency is manifested seductively, the more the games and pleasures of substitution occupy the attention of the gaze powerfully and captivate its desire, the less the mechanisms are noticed, the less they are acknowledged'[126]. The dream (or perhaps nightmare) of a medium achieving *absolute* transparency and of a user experiencing *total* immersion has yet to come true; that it will *never* come true, however, is another prophecy we would do better to question.

124 Peter Weibel, 'The Intelligent Image: Neurocinema or Quantum Cinema?', in *Future Cinema: The Cinematic Imaginary after Film*, ed. by Jeffrey Shaw and Peter Weibel (Cambridge MA–London: The MIT Press, 2003), pp. 594–601 (p. 599).

125 See Fabienne Liptay and Burcu Dogramaci (eds), *Immersion in the Visual Arts and Media* (Leiden–Boston: Brill Rodopi, 2016), p. 7.

126 Marin, 'The Frame of Representation and Some of Its Figures', p. 353.

III

FRAMELESS: THE ABSTRACT SUBLIME

1. *Ars Est Ostentare Artem*

By letting images escape their "natural habitat" and blend into flesh-bound reality or, on the contrary, by inviting the experiencer to enter the image-world, hyperrealism and immersivity seem to move in opposite directions. And yet, on closer inspection, they both use the same strategy to undermine the representational paradigm, that is, they both push representation to the point where it ends up negating itself. While *ontologically* being pictures, a wax statue or an immersive virtual reality environment tend to *phenomenologically* present themselves not as representational images, but as autonomous entities characterised by the same *presentness*, the same *immediateness*, and the same *unframedness* as everyday reality[1].

In so doing, hyperrealistic images and immersive environments corrode representation *from the inside*: they are both its apotheosis and its *reductio ad absurdum*. For while representation, by definition, implies a mediated experience, these types of images offer a semblance of non-mediateness, which is nevertheless obtained, paradoxically enough, by exploiting the technical or technological potential of the media involved to the fullest. Consider the ancient principle of *ars est celare artem*: taking it literally and in its most extreme sense would be denying *ars* itself, eliminating any elements that might reveal the arti-factual nature of all images. The attempt to circumvent the unavoidable

1 See Andrea Pinotti, 'Environmentalising the Image: Towards An-Iconology', *Screen*, forthcoming 2020.

mediateness of representation translates into an attempt to disguise the medium as an element that prevents illusion, understood here in the sense of perceptual deception.

Alongside this first strategy of undermining the dispositif of representation there is another one based on exactly the opposite principle. Instead of concealing the medium in order to turn representation into presentation, this second strategy highlights and emphasises it so as to free it from its traditional subservience to representation. In this case, the medium is seen not as an *obstacle* to illusion *qua* perceptual deception, but rather as an element that *favours* illusion *qua in-lusio* (that is, a game of representation, make-believe, pretence, and fiction). Undermining representation is contingent on ensuring that the medium *stops being a medium*: as soon as it ceases to mediate between the picture and the object it refers to, the medium is brought to the fore and magnified as an autonomous element that is meaningful in itself. The dispositif of representation is called into question because it is considered too illusionistic (as opposed to not illusionistic enough); consequently, the medium is not pushed towards maximum transparency but towards maximum opacity. *Ars est ostentare artem*.

This exhibition of the medium entails a radical denial of the whole technical and theoretical apparatus underlying the concept of representation as fiction, an idea that found its most evident expression in the traditional notion of the *picture*: 'The Western easel painting subordinates decorative to dramatic effect, cutting the illusion of a boxlike cavity into the wall behind it and organizing within this cavity the illusion of forms, light, and space, all more or less according to the current rules of verisimilitude'[2]. Since the beginning of the fifteenth century, pictures have been understood first of all as *objects*, and secondly, more specifically, as *representational* objects: isolated parts of an infinite world.

Inaugurated by Masaccio and Brunelleschi and theorised by Leon Battista Alberti, the dispositif of modern pictorial representation couples picture and representation in an

2 Clement Greenberg, 'The Crisis of the Easel Picture' (1948), in *The Collected Essays and Criticism*, ed. by John O'Brian, 4 vols (Chicago–London: The University of Chicago Press, 1986), II, pp. 221–25 (p. 221).

inseparable and apparently natural combination based on the following fundamental principles: pictures are imitations of the visible ('The painter strives to represent [*imitari*] only things that are visible under light'[3]); the plane of representation, as a "cut" into the visual pyramid, is a window onto the world ('What I myself do when I paint: first I trace as large a quadrangle as I wish, with right angles, on the surface to be painted; in this place, it certainly functions for me as an open window through which the historia is observed'[4]); and *historia* is 'the most important work of the painter, in which every richness and elegance of things must certainly be present'[5]. Representing the sphere of the visible within a space organised according to the laws of perspective, the picture turns out to be a construction aimed at simulating reality in the form of an iconic narrative: it is eminently *fiction*. Like theatre, painting is a dramatic art, capable of playing out verisimilar scenes that can be *read* as representations of reality, whether actual or fictional[6].

In order to be understood as a finite representation of a potentially unlimited visual field, the picture must appear as a cut into reality: 'When a relatively stable and seemingly natural mimetic space was set up in the fifteenth century, painting – which was no longer defined as the iconic symbolization of the divine, but as the plane imitation of the visible – had to start with a sharp cut within the visible itself'[7]. The dispositif described by Alberti, which would become a long-standing canon in Western painting and treatises on the topic, is based on the assumption that the representation of reality – its *mise en scène* – should start with a gesture of separation and delimitation establishing a caesura that is essential for something to be a 'picture' of something else: the "conventional" Renaissance frame is to be seen "as much a

3 Leon Battista Alberti, *On Painting: A New Translation and Critical Edition*, ed. and trans. by Rocco Sinisgalli (Cambridge: Cambridge University Press, 2011), p. 23.

4 *Ibid.*, p. 39.

5 *Ibid.*, p. 81.

6 Even when the *sujet* of a work of art is an imaginary reality, it is still represented according to criteria of verisimilitude inspired by reality in the flesh.

7 Jean-Claude Lebensztejn, 'A partir du cadre (vignettes)' (1987), in *Annexes – de l'oeuvre d'art* (Paris: La Part de l'Œil, 1999), pp. 181–223 (p. 191).

theoretical as a real object, presupposing a certain pictorial mode and defining a particular realm for something we now called "art"'[8].

The close 'association of picture and frame'[9] is, therefore, not at all accidental, since it derives from the very concept of representation. If representation means picture, picture means frame, the latter being 'one of the conditions of possibility for contemplating the picture, for reading it, and thus for interpreting it. [...] The framing of a picture is the semiotic condition of its visibility, but also of its readability [...]. The frame is not a passive agency of the icon: it is, in the pragmatic interaction between viewer and representation, one of the operators of the constitution of the picture as a visible object whose entire purpose is to be seen'[10]. The frame delimits the space of the picture and, together with it, the space of representation: it is the gatekeeper of the image world. To access this world, one needs a pass, so to speak, which ultimately amounts to adopting the right attitude – the attitude of as-if: 'All picture frames define the identity of the fiction'[11].

Rudolf Arnheim has effectively summarised the fundamental reasons behind the close link between picture and frame. First of all, the frame encourages the observer to look at what is seen in the picture 'not as a part of the world in which he lives and acts, but as a statement about that world, at which he looks from the outside – a representation of the viewer's world'[12]. Secondly, precisely because they are understood as representations of reality, modern Western pictures aim to create their own pictorial space, and this, in turn, requires 'more than simple separation from the environmental space, in which the picture dwells as a physical object. The separation is difficult to obtain without a frame that

8 Alison Wright, *Frame Work: Honour and Ornament in Italian Renaissance Art* (New Haven and London: Yale University Press), p. 10.

9 Ortega y Gasset, 'Meditations on the Frame', p. 187.

10 Louis Marin, 'Figures of Reception in Modern Representation in Painting' (1985), trans. by Catherine Porter, in *On Representation*, pp. 320–36 (p. 323; translation modified).

11 Stoichita, *The Self-Aware Image*, p. 90.

12 Rudolf Arnheim, 'Limits and Frames', in *The Power of the Center: A Study of Composition in the Visual Arts* (Berkeley: University of California Press, 1982), pp. 42–70 (p. 52). By the same Author, see also *Art and Visual Perception: A Psychology of the Creative Eye*, expanded and revised edition (Berkeley–Los Angeles–London: University of California Press, 1974), pp. 239–41.

overlaps the pictorial space'[13]. Finally, once a caesura is established between real space and pictorial space, the frame acts as a window through which one may look into the pictorial space, or as a 'figure' upon the picture plane *qua* 'ground':

> The picture space is perceived as continuing beneath and beyond the frame. How indispensable the frame is for such a picture can be seen when one looks at the reproduction of a painting printed on white paper. There the painting acts as figure lying on top of the white ground, which creates an awkward visual contradiction at the borders. The picture space is required by its nature to continue but instead is cut off by its own contours and thereby defined as a flat surface.[14]

As a matter of fact, at the end of the nineteenth century the traditional dispositif of representation, along with the theoretical principles underlying it, started to falter. The very idea of the picture as an illusionistic, three-dimensional space conceived of 'as a stage animated by visual incident'[15] was called into question. The picture ceased to be regarded as a window onto the pictorial world, while the medium, which until then had been constantly 'covered'[16] by the representational image, was left *un*covered: by losing its transparency, it became free to display nothing but itself. Lines no longer needed to be contours of figures, nuances were no longer enslaved to mimetic adherence to reality (becoming pure colours instead), and light effects no longer had to merely create a sense of volume in an attempt to model three-dimensional objects and figures.

The 'crisis of the easel picture', as Clement Greenberg once called it in a short and enlightening essay by the same name, also concerned the frame. Indeed, it could not be otherwise, given the crucial role the latter plays within the dispositif of representation. In 1886, Georges Seurat painted *Evening, Honfleur*, in which his *pointillisme* did not even spare the frame (fig. 12).

---

13 *Ibid.*, p. 55.

14 *Ibid.*, p. 56.

15 Clement Greenberg, 'Abstract and Representational' (1954), in *The Collected Essays and Criticism*, pp. 186–93 (p. 190).

16 On the concept of 'covering' or 'overlapping' (*Verdeckung*) see Husserl, *Phantasy and Image Consciousness*.

Fig. 12 – Georgers Seurat, *Evening, Honfleur* (1886).
The Museum of Modern Art, New York

To be sure, this was not the first example of how the borderline, liminal space of the frame could be invaded by painting; however, all previous experiments tended to *accentuate* the power of representation. From the ambiguous cucumber that seems to protrude out of Carlo Crivelli's *Annunciation with St Emidius* (1486) to the putto breaking forth from Pere Borrell del Caso's significantly titled artwork *Escaping Criticism* (1874), the crossing of the frame-threshold had always been a highly illusionistic 'expressive device'[17]. With Seurat, instead, the opposite is true. His painting extends beyond the boundaries of the canvas to include the frame. But rather than merely being part of the representational space, the frame itself becomes the place where colour is shown *in and for itself*, free from any subservience to the composition of the representational image. The space enclosed within the frame is still the realm of representation, where we see spots of colour

17 Schapiro, *On Some Problems in the Semiotics of Visual Art*, p. 11.

as shore, water, sky, clouds, or sunset. On the frame, though, the same colours are nothing but stains: while they still echo the chromatic range of representation, with darker colours in lower parts and lighter ones in upper sections, they do not count as an *extension of* the representation on the frame, but as an *abstraction from* it. The observer thus experiences a sort of optical shock. At first, the mosaic-like brushstrokes of pointillism are automatically assembled to form the image of an evening landscape. However, once the gaze shifts to the frame, these very same brushstrokes are seen for what they actually are: the effect is to liberate colour from its traditional enslavement to figurative representation. Then, in a sort of *après-coup*, this revelation eventually reverberates throughout the representation itself, for after having "discovered" colour, as such, on the frame, the observer looks back at the space inside the frame to "discover" the pictorial representation itself to be, after all, nothing other than a coloured surface. The medium is brought out, image consciousness yields to perception, and representation fades away.

Thus, Seurat 'unwittingly arrived at the notion of pure painting *überhaupt*. He himself seems not to have recognized it, but it was there, in his practice and in his theory. The emphasis of his system lay mostly upon the abstract elements of painting – tone, colour, mass, line. He was the first [...] to attack the concept of the easel painting as a window'[18]. Not coincidentally, Wassily Kandinsky's *Glass Painting with the Sun (Small Pleasures)* – a picture dated 1910, the year of the first abstract watercolour – appears to be perfectly in line with Seurat's work, in that it too shows colour overflowing onto the frame, free from the duty of representation to which it is instead subjected *within* the painting: "When the frame becomes an integral part of the painting, it no longer functions as frame meant to represent the 'painting'. It has itself become an integral element of the aesthetic object and now helps to liberate it from the rule of representation"[19].

---

18 Clement Greenberg, 'Seurat, Science, and Art: Review of *Georges Seurat* by John Rewald' (1943), in *The Collected Essays and Criticism*, I, pp. 167-70 (p. 168).

19 Harries, *The Broken Frame*, p. 84.

The late work of Claude Monet ushered in a new crucial stage on this journey toward *dis*-illusion. Characterised by the absence of focalising centres and completely obfuscating the boundaries of representation, the *Water Lilies* series at the Orangerie, painted between 1914 and 1926, inaugurated the so-called 'all-over' composition. These boundaries are still materially present in the form of the canvas edges. However, the canvases themselves assume gigantic dimensions, hence being able to accommodate the various elements of the representation in fully realistic proportions: the pond, water lilies, and flowers, look like 'huge close-ups'[20] that, if seen from up close, make the visual field of the beholder literally "close up", engulfed by a sea of colour.

The *Water Lilies* paintings are all framed, but in relation to the size of the painted surfaces, the frames become essentially invisible. Deprived of their ordinary function, they are still there only as a vestige of a now outdated concept of representation. With the undermining of the traditional principle of illusion came the end of the picture as a window onto the world.

2. *Pictures vs Paintings*

In order to understand what happened to the framed picture once its age-old association with the principles of pictorial representation was disentangled, we need to move from Europe to the United States. There, around the mid-twentieth century, the revolutionary views of the later Monet began to be enthusiastically rediscovered by several American artists who were to become 'the most advanced of advanced painters'[21]. Regardless of their many individual differences, the works of the so-called abstract expressionists, and, in particular, of the main exponents of action and colour field painting, seem to have shared a staunch rejection of the whole dispositif of representation and, together with it, of the traditional meaning of the picture.

---

20 Clement Greenberg, 'The Later Monet' (1959), in *Art and Culture: Critical Essays* (Boston: Beacon Press, 1961), pp. 37–45 (p. 45).

21 *Ibid.*

Undoubtedly the most important theorist among all the leading figures of Abstract Expressionism, Barnett Newman explained the meaning of this rejection. In an interview with Lane Slate, the painter retraced his artistic career: 'It is hard to say what one has accomplished. The work speaks for itself. However, one of the things that can be said is that I helped change painting from the making of *pictures* to the making of *paintings*'[22]. The distinction between these two terms, which are often used interchangeably but are only apparently synonymous, runs as a leitmotif through many of Newman's writings. In a little-known essay entirely devoted to the work of the New York artist, Arthur Danto clarifies it further:

> A picture creates an illusory space, within which various objects are represented. The viewer, as it were, looks through the surface of a picture, as if through a window, into a virtual space, in which various objects are deployed and composed: the Virgin and Child surrounded by saints in an adoration; stripes surrounded by squiggles in an abstraction. In the Renaissance, a picture was regarded as transparent, so to speak, the way the front of the stage is, through which we see men and women caught up in actions that we know are not occurring in the space we ourselves occupy. In a painting, by contrast, the surface is opaque, like a wall. We are not supposed to see through it. We stand in a real relationship with it, rather than in an illusory relationship with what it represents. [...] A picture represents something other than itself; a painting presents itself. A picture mediates between a viewer and an object in pictorial space; a painting is an object to which the viewer relates without mediation.[23]

The opposition between picture and painting corresponds to the contrast between transparency and opacity, illusion and reality, representation and presentation, mediateness and immediateness – but not between abstract and figurative. Danto states it clearly: a picture can, indeed, also be abstract. Newman

22 Barnett Newman, 'Interview with Lane Slate' (1963), in *Selected Writings and Interviews*, ed. by John P. O'Neill, Text Notes and Commentary by Mollie McNickle, intro. by Richard Shiff (Berkeley–Los Angeles: University of California Press, 1992), pp. 251–54 (p. 253; emphasis added).

23 Arthur C. Danto, 'Barnett Newman and the Heroic Sublime', The Nation, 16 June 2002, 25–29 (p. 26).

himself is unequivocal on this point: 'Those who make pictures, *whether realistic or abstract*, are not making paintings'[24].

Reducing the distinction between picture and painting to that between figuration and abstraction would mean drawing a merely formal distinction, linked solely to the type of "language" the artist chooses to use; for Newman, instead, the opposition still arises, but it concerns, above all, *contents*. Further in the interview with Slate, the artist argues that his second fundamental achievement was to remove 'the nonobjective from nonobjective art', thus giving abstract art 'the possibility of a new set of human subjects'[25]. The opposition between abstract art and figurative art gives way to an opposition that is inherent in abstract art itself: one kind of abstraction, although employing abstract forms, continues to refer to traditional contents, whereas the other kind adopts an abstract language to convey entirely new contents – *abstract contents*.

In a conversation with Thomas Hess, Newman declared peremptorily: 'The history of my generation begins with the problem of what to paint'[26]. *What*, not *how* to paint. According to Newman, the "language" of contemporary art could only be that of abstraction, but abstraction itself had to be transformed into something completely different from what it had been so far: 'The insistence of the abstract artists that subject matter be eliminated, that art be made pure, has served to create a result similar to that in Mohammedan art, which insisted on eliminating anthropomorphic shapes. Both fanaticisms, which strive toward an abstract purity, force the art to become a mere arabesque'[27].

The key word, in this case, is *subject matter*. The attempt to definitively sever all ties with a thousand-year-old pictorial tradition that, although using radically different schemes, was still aimed at translating the outside world into image, resulted in so-called "pure" art, which however completely failed to break the mimetic spell of representation:

---

24 Newman, 'Interview with Lane Slate', p. 253 (emphasis added).

25 Ibid, p. 254.

26 Barnett Newman, 'A Conversation: Barnett Newman and Thomas Hess' (1966), in *Selected Writings and Interviews*, pp. 273–86 (p. 274).

27 Barnett Newman, 'The Plasmic Image' (1945), in *Selected Writings and Interviews*, pp. 138–55 (p. 141).

> The purists tried to deny nature and became involved with its diagrammatic equivalents – with the realism of geometric shapes. A ninety-degree angle, a triangle and a circle are as much a part of nature as a tree and have all its elements of recognizability. In truth, the purists, from Mondrian to Kandinsky, never denied nature but asserted they were depicting the truest nature, the nature of mathematical law. [...] Mondrian, no matter how formally pure his abstraction, creates a diagrammatic world which is the geometric equivalent for the seen landscape, the vertical trees on a horizon, and we are brought into the world of material purity through a representational depiction of its mathematical equivalents.[28]

Representational depiction: from Newman's perspective, Kandinsky, and especially Mondrian, had transfigured the real world into a geometric-ideal world of pure forms and colours, but without actually succeeding in emancipating themselves from the representative injunction. The whole dispositif of representation is based on the assumption that images are always images-of, in the sense that they depict something that is not itself an image. From this point of view, representation is synonymous with depiction, a term that inevitably connotes 'picture'. The theoretical issue is the same: to provide 'individually necessary and jointly sufficient conditions for being a picture of some object'[29].

This same issue was also central to early twentieth-century abstractionism. For Newman and his fellow abstract expressionists, overcoming the dispositif of representation necessarily involved

28 Barnett Newman, 'Response to Clement Greenberg' (1947), in *Selected Writings and Interviews*, pp. 161–64 (p. 163). A similar view would be later developed by Meyer Schapiro, again in relation to Mondrian's work: 'In abstract painting the system of marks, strokes and spots and certain ways of combining and distributing them on the field have become available for arbitrary use without the requirement of correspondence as signs. The forms that result are not simplified abstracted forms of objects; yet the elements applied in a non-mimetic, uninterpreted whole retain many of the qualities of and formal relationships of the preceding mimetic art. [...] The conception of the picture-field as corresponding in its entirety to a segment of space excerpted from a larger whole is preserved in abstract painting' (Meyer Schapiro, *On Some Problems in the Semiotics of Visual Arts*, pp. 18-19).

29 Catharine Abell and Katerina Bantinaki (eds), *Philosophical Perspectives on Depiction* (Oxford–New York: Oxford University Press, 2010), p. 2.

surmounting this first form of abstractionism. What was needed was a transition 'from abstract *language* to abstract *thought*', from 'abstract disciplines' to 'abstract subject matter'[30]. Abstract art was in need of new *contents*:

> There is a difference between a purist art and an art form used purely. In the former, the result is a formal pattern which, separated from the emotional excitement that accompanies insight or revelation, is objective, cold, impersonal, and consequently incapable of giving complete satisfaction to the intensity generated by man's spiritual need. The best that can be said for this type of art is that it is decorative, that it satisfies man's taste for "beauty." There has been a great to-do lately over Mondrian's genius. His point of view, his fanatic purism, is the matrix of the abstract aesthetic. His concept, however, is founded on bad philosophy and on faulty logic.[31]

Here, Newman makes another crucial point: 'picture' and 'representation' go hand in hand with 'beauty', understood as the ideal goal of art since the days of classical Greece. The *sujet* of the work can certainly be, in itself, ugly or disgusting, as in the famous case of Chardin's *Ray*; its representation, though, still refers to the paradigm of beauty – it remains a *beautiful representation* of an *ugly subject matter*. This ideal of beauty as the ultimate goal of art had even survived the formal revolution of early twentieth-century abstract painting, which, despite appearances, was still linked to the traditional notion of the picture as the formal composition and arrangement of a scene.

Newman's criticism of this kind of abstraction would be reiterated by the next generation of American artists, particularly the exponents of Minimalism. In an interview with Bruce Glaser, Frank Stella and Donald Judd echoed Newman's parallel between picture, beauty, and composition, describing the work of Kandinsky and Mondrian in a language verging on contempt: 'The European geometric painters really strive for what I call relational painting.

30 Barnett Newman, 'Teresa Zarnower' (1946), in *Selected Writings and Interviews*, pp. 103–05 (p. 105).
31 Barnett Newman, 'The Plasmic Image', pp. 140-41.

The basis of their whole idea is balance. You do something in one corner and you balance it with something in the other'[32].

Newman discovered the alternative to the ideal of beauty and to the related principles of form, composition, staging, illusion, and fiction on the day of his forty-third birthday, on 29 January 1948, the day he painted *Onement I*. He would later say that, in creating this artwork, he felt that 'for the first time there was no picture making'[33]. So what is so special about *Onement I*, given that its modest size would still seem to connect it to traditional easel painting? First of all, in no way can it be interpreted as a representation (not even in the sense of a remote abstraction) of some natural subject matter. Secondly, the use of a single vertical band (Newman's famous 'zip'), linking together violently juxtaposed areas of strong colour, eliminated any reference whatsoever to the traditional relationship between a dominant figure and the recessive ground. It was not the first time Newman deployed an apparently similar formal pattern, but until that juncture, the zip had always looked as if it were standing in front of some background colour that could be conceived 'as natural atmosphere'[34]. Last, but not least, *Onement I* breaks all ties with the European tradition of formally "arranging" the picture as a stage: the vertical zip is not "balanced" by any horizontal line, and there is no "harmonisation" of cool with warm colours.

These characteristics distinguish *Onement I* from all previous artworks not only from a formal point of view, but also in terms of contents: what is being questioned, or rather undermined, is the entire traditional aesthetics based on the representational paradigm. For Newman and the other abstract expressionists, this definitive refusal to recognise beauty as the ultimate goal of art *qua* art was an epoch-making change, a revolution marking a shift in the centre of gravity of the art world from Europe to the United

32 Stella's answer to Glaser, 'Questions to Stella and Judd' (1966), in *Minimal Art: A Critical Anthology*, ed. by Gregory Battcock, intro. by Anne M. Wagner (Berkeley–Los Angeles–London: University of California Press, 1995), pp. 148–64 (p. 149).

33 Newman interviewed by Emile de Antonio in 1970, in *Selected Writings and Interviews*, pp. 302–08 (p. 306).

34 Barnett Newman, *Interview with David Sylvester* (1965), in *Selected Writings and Interviews*, pp. 254–59 (p. 255).

States. And yet, paradoxically enough, in order to find a concept capable of replacing beauty and providing abstract art with new contents (that is, with a new subject matter), Newman had to return to the European tradition. In the same year in which he painted *Onement I*, he also wrote an essay of capital importance whose title, *The Sublime Is Now*, speaks for itself:

> Modern art, caught without a sublime content, was incapable of creating a new sublime image and, unable to move away from the Renaissance imagery of figures and objects except by distortion or by denying it completely for an empty world of geometric formalisms – a pure rhetoric of abstract mathematical relationships – became enmeshed in a struggle over the nature of beauty: whether beauty was in nature or could be found without nature.
>
> I believe that here in America, some of us, free from the weight of European culture, are finding the answer, by completely denying that art has any concern with the problem of beauty and where to find it. The question that now arises is how, if we are living in a time without a legend or mythos that can be called sublime, if we refuse to admit any exaltation in pure relations, if we refuse to live in the abstract, how can we be creating a sublime art?[35]

In Newman's reasoning, the new abstract art is not a non-objective art form: rather, it has its own specific object – the sublime. Newman makes reference to some of the most prominent philosophers who, between the eighteenth and nineteenth centuries, had investigated the enigmatic, paradoxical 'mixed feeling' of 'delightful horror' or 'negative pleasure' that is set against beauty like formlessness is set against form, measurelessness against measure, indeterminacy against determinacy. The central theoretical tenet is that the sublime, unlike the beautiful, is not an objective property but a subjective feeling. And this is where the distinction between picture and painting overlaps with the traditional opposition between beautiful and sublime. While a picture creates its own pictorial space in which certain objects are represented, a painting presents itself in our own space and time. This means that while

35 Barnett Newman, 'The Sublime Is Now' (1948), in *Selected Writings and Interviews*, pp. 170–73 (p. 173).

a picture is a beautiful representation made to be seen, "read", and interpreted, a painting is a sublime presentation made to be experienced: as another champion of Abstract Expressionism, Mark Rothko, put it, 'a painting is not a picture of an experience; it is an experience'[36].

If the sublime, by definition, is what exceeds representation, and if representation is synonymous with picture, then the sublime is what denies the very essence of the picture. This syllogistic reasoning also applies to the frame: *if picture means frame, no picture means no frame*. There is a small but significant episode that may shed light on this fundamental aspect of the rejection of representation. In a letter addressed to the director of the Guggenheim Museum James Johnson Sweeney, and also sent to the *New York Times*, Newman argued against the idea of exhibiting some great artworks by Picasso, Braque, Mirò, and Cézanne 'stripped of their frames'. According to the New York painter, it was a historically misleading attempt to bring modern art and contemporary art closer together: 'I, as one of the first painters to reject the frame, feel that any presentation of my own pictures in a frame would, in effect, mutilate them. However, I feel that it is just as mutilating to show Cezanne without a frame'[37].

It is a curious and extremely significant fact that Newman interpreted the possible framing of his works – which are for the most part frameless[38] – as a dangerous form of *mutilation*. Mutilation involves taking away: an organic whole is violently deprived of one or more parts. In Cézanne's case, it is therefore perfectly intuitive to understand what Newman means: removing the frame from one of his pictures means depriving it of an element essential to the picture *qua* picture. In Newman's works, however, it would not be a matter of taking away, but rather of *adding* something, namely the frame. But how could addition be understood as mutilation? To answer this question, let us refer to an observation made by Greenberg that pushes the opposition

36 Mark Rothko interviewed by Dorothy Seiberling, Life, 16 November 1959, p. 82.

37 Barnett Newman, 'Letter to the Editor', The New York Times Magazine, 7 June 1954, in *Selected Writings and Interviews*, pp. 40–41 (p. 41).

38 For the very rare cases in which Newman chose to frame his paintings, see Yve-Alain Bois, '*The Wild* and Company', *October*, 143 (2013), pp. 95–125.

between picture and painting even further. While in Kandinsky's paintings the pictorial surface still remains 'a mere receptacle'[39], an abstract expressionist painting is no longer '"packaged", wrapped up and sealed in, to declare it as easel painting'[40]. An image that is no longer a receptacle no longer needs to be contained; therefore, framing it would mean mutilating it, violently circumscribing something that demands instead to be apprehended 'less as a receptacle given in advance than as open field'[41].

In a sense, this 'open field' also characterises many of Mondrian's works, which can be interpreted as finite portions of geometric grids to be infinitely extended in the imagination of the observer. Indeed, it was Mondrian who declared himself the first artist 'to bring the painting forward from the frame, rather than set it within the frame', having noted that 'a picture without a frame works better than a framed one'[42]. His aim, he maintained, was to get rid of the 'sensations of three dimensions', the 'illusion of depth'[43] that had always been so closely linked to the frame. To be sure, Mondrian's works played a crucial role in a process based on the following principle: 'The less illusionistic the image, the more inessential the frame'[44]. Schapiro further elaborated on this theme:

> More recently paintings have been hung altogether unframed. The frameless modern picture explains in a sense the functions of the frame in older art. The frame was dispensable when painting ceased to represent deep space and became more concerned with the expressive and formal qualities of the non-mimetic marks than with their elaboration into signs. If the painting once receded within the framed space, the canvas now stands out from the wall as an

---

39 Clement Greenberg, 'Kandinsky' (1948, 1957), in *Art and Culture*, pp. 111–14 (113).

40 Clement Greenberg, 'Contribution to a Symposium' (1953), in *Art and Culture*, pp. 124–26 (p. 124).

41 *Ibid.*

42 Piet Mondrian, 'An Interview with Mondrian' by James Johnson Sweeney, in *Eleven Europeans in America, The Museum of Modern Art Bulletin*, 13, 4–5 (1946), pp. 35–36.

43 Piet Mondrian interviewed by James Johnson Sweeney, 'An Interview with Mondrian', in *Piet Mondrian: Exhibition Catalogue* (New York: Museum of Modern Art, 1948), pp. 1–16 (p. 15).

44 Zaloscer, 'Versuch einer Phänomenologie des Rahmens', p. 217.

> object in its own right, with a tangibly painted surface whether of abstract themes or with a representation which is predominantly flat and shows the activity of the artist in the pronounced lines and strokes or the high arbitrariness of the selected forms and colors.[45]

The need for 'flatness' as an essential tool for circumventing pictorial illusion links the work of Mondrian to that of many abstract expressionists, but this is as far as the analogy goes. The elimination of the frame, in particular, responds to different needs and different objectives. While the pictures of the Dutch painter simply 'work worse' when framed, the paintings of Newman, Rothko, or Pollock do not work at all. Arnheim notes that a frame 'is not just a fence demarking the range of the picture', because it also acts 'as a compositional center, attracting or repelling components of the picture'. This power of the frame, though, presupposes that the picture contains 'definite visual objects'. If, instead, it presents 'a fairly even texture, as occurs in the paintings of the abstract expressionists', then the frame 'cannot get a handle on the picture, for the reason that the frame acts essentially through the verticality and horizontality of its four sides'. It supplies 'the Cartesian coordinates that the artist otherwise might have to represent within his design'[46].

Now, this is exactly what Mondrian does: he offers the viewer a geometrical pattern to indicate 'the Cartesian coordinates' of representation. The Dutch artist's works remain pictures in that they are shaped as perfectly regular and balanced cut-outs in which the viewer can easily orient themselves: the canvas, as geometrically simplified and balanced as it is, still presents itself as 'the *scene* of forms rather than as one single, indivisible piece of texture'[47]. Newman's paintings, on the other hand, are designed to disorient those who observe (or rather, *experience*) them. His famous zips do not delimit or balance anything: they are not meant to fit into a composition, but, on the contrary, to overcome the very idea of composition and, together with it, the idea of beauty.

45 Schapiro, 'On Some Problems in the Semiotics of Visual Arts', p. 98.
46 Arnheim, *The Power of the Centre*, p. 59.
47 Greenberg, 'The Crisis of the Easel Picture', p. 223.

The zips are the concrete manifestation – the embodiment – of the sublime, that is, of disorientation at its purest.

For Newman and colleagues, then, discarding the frame means rejecting the packaging, the perfect balancing, the orientation, that is, the whole *architecture* that, for centuries, seemed to be a necessary condition of painting *qua* the creation of pictures. The frame must be abandoned when the artist seeks to eliminate all the elements that interpose and mediate between the real space and the illusory space to which representational images essentially belong. Ortega maintained that a picture without a frame looks like 'a naked, despoiled man', its contents seeming 'to spill out over the four sides of the canvas and dissolve into the atmosphere'[48]. It is as if Newman and colleagues reinterpreted these words by giving them a *positive* meaning. In order to overcome the traditional notion of pictorial representation and the theoretical apparatus it was built upon, the canvas must indeed 'dissolve into the atmosphere': the picture had to turn into an environment, the observer into an experiencer.

3. *Vir Heroicus Sublimis*

Princeton, February 1961. Among the numerous letters, envelopes, and packages filling his desk, an almost seventy-year-old Erwin Panofsky notices the latest issue of *ARTnews*, a journal founded in 1902 that quickly became one of the most prestigious mouthpieces of the contemporary art scene. While casually leafing through the pages, he finds an enthusiastic review of his recently released book, *Renaissance and Renascences in Western Art*, penned by art critic George Kubler[49]. Intrigued, he starts reading and discovers that, instead of the usual homage to an undisputed *auctoritas*, the brief essay was an attempt to reconsider some fundamental concepts of his work in order to apply them to 1940s and 1950s American art. Kubler had taken his cue, in particular, from the famous 'law of disjunction' between forms and

48 Ortega y Gasset, 'Meditations on the Frame', p. 187.
49 George Kubler, 'Disjunction and Mutational Energy', *ARTnews*, 60, 1 (1961), 34 and 55.

meanings that distinguishes, according to Panofsky, the medieval 'renascences' with respect to the Renaissance proper: 'Wherever a sculptor or painter borrows a figure or a group from a classical work of art he almost invariably invests it with a non-classical, viz., Christian, meaning; conversely, wherever he borrows a theme from classical poetry, mythology, or history he almost invariably presents it in a non-classical, viz., contemporary form'[50].

Although it is hard to determine whether he was fully aware of the theoretical change with respect to Panofsky's initial idea, the reviewer replaced this original formulation of the concept of 'disjunction' with an alternative, considered to be typical of contemporary American art. This new formulation was based on the assumption that the Abstract Expressionism's rejection of traditional European *forms* could also bring about a radical change in the *meanings* to which those forms had been giving shape for centuries. While Panofsky's principle of 'disjunction' entailed either the persistence of a certain form to express a different meaning or, vice versa, the persistence of a certain meaning expressed in different forms, Kubler argued that the Abstract Expressionism's demise of traditional formal values could bring with it the annihilation of traditional content-related values and the subsequent creation of completely new forms and contents, thereby inaugurating nothing less than a new Renaissance in art and culture. In Kubler's opinion, following in the footsteps of Athens, Florence, and Paris, it was now up to New York to take on the role of world capital of art. Precisely from this perspective, *Renaissance and Renascences* could be regarded as 'a signpost in the difficult reorientation that our actual periodological change requires'[51].

Faced with such an attempt to "update" his own theories, Panofsky responds with subtle ambiguity in a letter to the Director of *ARTnews*, Henry La Farge. While expressing gratitude for the kind words about his work, he also voices a concern that those very same words 'seem to encourage contemporary artists to read my book or even to invest the outrageous sum of 19 dollars in

50 Erwin Panofsky, *Renaissance and Renascences in Western Art* (1960) (New York: Harper & Row, 1972), p. 25.

51 Kubler, 'Disjunction and Mutational Energy', p. 34.

it... because it is really directed only to what a less well-meaning colleague has called "the pedants"'[52]. The irony is so explicit that, reading between the lines, one can easily imagine the Princeton professor's sarcastic grimace. By inferring the price of *Renaissance and Renascences* to be 'outrageous', Panofsky's intention is obviously not to belittle the value of his book; rather, with skilled rhetoric, he pretends to put himself in the shoes of the contemporary artists Kubler's review was intended for, claiming – *contra* Kubler himself – that in their eyes the book would not be worth the cost. He then includes himself, with feigned modesty, among the 'pedants', that is, his own colleagues, the art historians, thus claiming the book to be conceived specifically and solely for them. Thus, while formally offering his thanks for the review, Panofsky cryptically contests its fundamental assumption, protesting against Kubler's attempt to extend the validity of his own analysis to the artistic movements that had taken hold in post-World War II America.

The real target concealed behind what amounts to a clear-cut (albeit expressed with gentle irony) bashing of Kubler's thesis emerges even more clearly further on in the letter. Pulling off his mask and the 'pedant' disguise, Panofsky retaliates against those artists who might consider the price of *Renaissance and Renascences* unreasonable:

> I find it increasingly hard to keep up with contemporary art, particularly with the titles affixed to some of the objects. A signal example has appeared in the current number of *ARTnews* [February 1961] where Mr. Barnett Newman's composition is entitled *Vir Heroicus Sublimus*. I find myself confronted with three different interpretations of the curious form 'Sublimus': does Mr. Newman imply that he, as Aelfric says of God, is 'above grammar'; or is it a misprint; or is it plain illiteracy? In the optimistic assumption that the first of these possible interpretations is true, and with my best thanks...[53]

He finally signs the letter, not forgetting to present his work address in plain view and singling out each word 'as if wanting

52 Erwin Panofsky, 'Letter to H.A. La Farge' (20 February 1961), *ARTnews*, 60, 2 (April), 6. Reprinted in Erwin Panofsky, *Korrespondenz 1957 bis 1961*, ed. by Dieter Wuttke (Wiesbaden: Harrassowitz, 2008), pp. 872–73.

53 Panofsky, 'Letter to H.A. La Farge', p. 6.

to dot the i's and cross the t's'[54] in proud reclamation of an almost guild-like, corporative membership: 'Erwin Panofsky, The Institute for Advanced Study, Princeton'. The German-American scholar exploited a simple review to differentiate between his cultural *milieu* and that of contemporary artists, regarded not only as foreign to his own, but also as frivolous and trivial. Indeed, we should not gloss over the fact that Panofsky merely refers to what are widely considered masterpieces of Abstract Expressionism as 'objects'. In this undeniably negative value judgement, which clearly reveals Panofsky's polemical attitude, such works are just things, colour-sodden surfaces, no more sophisticated than the canvases "painted" by Betsy, the chimpanzee who made headlines in the late 1950s for her alleged artistic skills and the purported resemblance between her "style" and that of some American abstract artists[55].

Panofsky explicitly mentions the Betsy case in two letters, both dated November 1958. In the first, a reply to the Hungarian art theorist György Kepes who had invited him to publish an essay on 'Visual Arts Today', he claims that, in so far as contemporary art is concerned[56], he can only refer to Betsy's work, the implicit suggestion being that he in fact found no difference at all between her works and those of the abstract artists. In the second letter, written to a young PhD student, Panofsky cuts to the chase, declaring that 'there is, in fact, no methodical possibility of distinguishing the productions of Betsy from those of, let us say, Mr. Jackson Pollock'[57].

54 Beat Wyss, *Ein Druckfehler: Panofsky versus Newman – Verpasste Chancen eines Dialogs* (Köln: König, 1993), p. 6.

55 See on this Horst Waldemar Janson, 'After Betsy, What?', *Bulletin of the Atomic Scientists*, 15, 2 (1959), 68–71 and 93; Desmond Morris, *The Biology of Art: A Study of the Picture-Making Behaviour of the Great Apes and Its Relationship to Human Art* (London: Methuen, 1962); Thierry Lenain, *La peinture des singes : Histoire et esthétique*, pref. by Desmond Morris (Paris: Syros–Alternatives, 1990).

56 Erwin Panofsky, 'Letter to G. Kepes' (11 November 1958), in Panofsky, *Korrespondenz 1957 bis 1961*, pp. 357–58 (p. 357).

57 Erwin Panofsky, 'Letter to W.H. Woody Jr.' (14 November 1958), in *Korrespondenz 1957 bis 1961*, pp. 358–62 (p. 359). Similar in content Panofsky's 'Letter to W.S. Heckscher', 22 April 1957, in *Korrespondenz 1957 bis 1961*, pp. 95–96.

Given the above, it is not hard to imagine that a review of *Renaissance and Renascences* in the most widely circulated contemporary art journal of the day could not but irk the peevish Princeton professor, who as early as September 1959 had expressed to his friend John Canaday his conviction that he was not as stuck in the past or as 'reactionary' as 'the readers, editors, and advertisers of *ARTnews*' might assume[58]. In short, the relationship between the professor and the magazine's staff was star-crossed – the kind that starts off badly and ends up even worse.

Indeed, this is how it went. Although Panofsky's letter to La Farge was not meant for publication, it did appear (although in a slightly shortened form) in the following issue of the journal[59], perhaps due to a banal oversight (as the editor of *ARTnews* Alfred Frankfurter maintained, apologising for the negligence)[60] or rather, much more likely, owing to a deliberate move. It was Barnett Newman himself who promptly replied, bringing out his consummate skills as a polemicist to score a swift blow in response. With more than a hint of sarcasm, he is quick to clarify that the form *sublimus* Panofsky was so upset by – incorrectly employed in the caption to a picture reproducing *Vir Heroicus Sublimis* included in a short essay by Robert Rosenblum, *The Abstract Sublime*[61], which appeared in the very same issue of *ARTnews* along with Kubler's review – was nothing other than a simple typo:

> Had Panofsky read the article, it would have been obvious to him that it is a misprint because in Prof. Rosenblum's article, the word is spelled as I intended it, *Sublimis*. Only in the caption is it *Sublimus*. Were I to follow the Panofskian dialectic, I could charge that he is above reading the text, or that he did not read, or that he cannot read. I shall not, however, stoop to the Panofskian techniques in order to

58 Erwin Panofsky, 'Letter to J. Canaday' (17 September 1959), in *Korrespondenz 1957 bis 1961*, pp. 526–28 (p. 527).

59 *ARTnews*, 60, 2 (April 1961), 6.

60 See Frankfurter's 'Letter to E. Panofsky' (9 August 1961), in Panofsky, *Korrespondenz 1957 bis 1961*, p. 1003, as well as Panofsky's clearly irritated reply of 18 August 1961 ('Letter to A. Frankfurter', in *Korrespondenz 1957 bis 1961*, p. 1010).

61 Robert Rosenblum, 'The Abstract Sublime', *ARTnews*, 60, 1 (February 1961), 39–40 and 56–58.

> hope that the third of these is true. I shall be generous enough to believe that he attacked me without reading the text.[62]

Resorting to the same logic as the eminent professor, Newman points out the arrogance of his critic, who did not even bother to read Rosenblum's essay, focusing solely on the caption and exploiting it as a pretext to castigate modern art practice. But there is more. Thanks to his great erudition, Newman cautions against assuming the form *sublimus* to be grammatically incorrect. Supporting his argument with references to Accius and Cicero, he demonstrates (with the help of such a unique 'prompter'[63] as Meyer Schapiro) the variant to be just as legitimate as the more commonly used term. Finally – and this is what interests us here the most – the letter ends with the statement that 'for a work of art to be a work of art, it must rise above grammar and syntax – *pro gloria Dei*'[64]. Here is the theoretical crux proper: Newman blames Panofsky for having speciously dwelled upon a minor, negligible issue, a matter of mere form, without being able or willing to understand the needs and feelings shared by the abstract expressionists.

The reply from Princeton that came shortly afterwards was rather surprising, in that it seemed to take no notice of the many important issues Newman raised and kept the focus on grammar. While admitting that the form *sublimus* did indeed exist, Panofsky nonetheless argued that it could only refer to concrete objects or phenomena occupying an elevated position in space, not to abstract notions or human beings. Therefore, even though grammatically acceptable, the variant of the word – notwithstanding Newman's alleged knowledge of Latin – was used in the wrong context. The closing is stinging: 'When I am shown a classical author using such *juncturae* as *homo sublimus*, *vir sublimus*, or *heroes sublimi*, I shall extend my apologies

62 Barnett Newman, 'Letter to A. Frankfurter', *ARTnews*, 60, 3 (May 1961), 6. Reprinted in Panofsky, *Korrespondenz 1957 bis 1961*, pp. 931–32.

63 In a letter dating from the Spring of 1961, Newman thanks Schapiro for his '"sublime" help' against Panofsky (Newman, *Selected Writings and Interviews*, p. 218). See Beat Wyss, 'La contemporaneità di un medievista: il suggeritore dell'artista', in *Meyer Schapiro e i metodi della storia dell'arte*, ed. by Luca Bortolotti *et al.* (Milan: Mimesis, 2010), pp. 89–103.

64 Newman, 'Letter to A. Frankfurter', p. 6.

to the compositors and proof-readers of *ARTnews* and shall be glad to think of Mr. Newman as a *pictor sublimus*'[65].

Prior to its publication, Panofsky's letter reached Newman, giving him ample time to conceive a new reply for inclusion in the same issue of the journal. Although at first sticking to the linguistic aspects of the controversy, Newman eventually strikes at the heart of the problem by criticising the professor (now declassed to 'doctor') for having surreptitiously transformed what was initially a matter of *grammar* into a different problem concerning *style*. But even in the case of this argument, Newman remained unconvinced, noting that *sublimus* could surely also be used – contrary to Panofsky's assumption – to describe a human being in the context of an elevated, archaic style. Yet it is clear that, for Newman, the grammar-semantic diatribe that seemed to excite the Princeton professor was nothing more than a boring pastime for learned scholars, only useful for diverting attention from the key point, which was the attempt 'to deny the artist's right to create poetic language, the right of *potestas audendi*'[66]. This is a subtle but crucial move, as the discourse is transposed from a simply linguistic level to a far more important matter concerning art: Newman claims the right to "poetic licence" both in the context of using archaic terms and in disclosing new paths for the visual arts. Art has never been a question of mere grammar, and it should never slavishly conform to pre-established vocabularies or specific rules. On the contrary, it is *poiesis*, that is, the creation of new vocabularies and new rules that modify or even overturn previous canons and perspectives.

Newman's move proved to be checkmate for his opponent. Instead of answering the legitimate questions raised by the artist, Panofsky chose to focus on the pedantry of grammar as if in a

65 Erwin Panofsky, 'Letter to A. Frankfurter', *ARTnews*, 60, 5 (September 1961), 6. Reprinted in Panofsky, *Korrespondenz 1957 bis 1961*, pp. 956–57. I do not agree with Beat Wyss when he argues that Panofsky's words were just a kind of benevolent appreciation of Newman's work expressed 'in a breezy tone to achieve a peaceful settlement of the controversy' (Wyss, *Ein Druckfehler*, p. 10). Similar words are also to be found in Wyss, 'Meyer Schapiro', p. 93.

66 Barnett Newman, 'Letter to A. Frankfurter', *ARTnews*, 60, 5 (September 1961), 6. Reprinted in Panofsky, *Korrespondenz 1957 bis 1961*, pp. 1016–19, as well as in Newman, *Selected Writings and Interviews*, pp. 219–20.

spelling competition. Reluctantly, Newman accepted a challenge he had no interest in, quarrelling on what he considered an absolutely trivial subject and an irrelevant aspect of the question at hand. Crucially, however, he also seized the opportunity to stress what he truly cared about, namely the high value of contemporary art practice: 'I hope that he [Panofsky] is not convinced for to be called *pictor sublimis* or *sublimus* by one who has consistently shown himself to be unfeeling towards any work of art since Dürer is too much'[67]. Tellingly, Panofsky never replied.

What might at first glance seem like a marginal episode in the history of the frequently fraught relations between artists on the one hand and art historians and theorists on the other is, in fact, a complex and delicate matter, namely whether or not iconology – in the modern, Panofskian sense of the word – can be applied to abstract art. Panofsky's tripartite art-historical approach prescribes that if the formal elements of an image do not allow the viewer to single out any mimetically reproduced *sujet* (be it a mountain, animal, or human being), then the basic level of pre-iconographic identification is precluded. This, in turn, makes it impossible to reach the second level of iconography: here the viewer, on the basis of her knowledge of one or more texts, gives a name to the subject portrayed, identifying the 'stories and allegories'[68] at the core of the work. Yet without this second step it is also hard to imagine how to reach the third and final level of art analysis, that of iconology, which focuses on the fact that any particular representation is based on principles that reveal 'the basic attitude of a nation, a period, a class, a religious or philosophical persuasion – qualified by one personality and condensed into one work'[69].

The existence and extent of the problem are demonstrated by the almost complete lack of references to non-objective and non-representational art within Panofsky's published works. Franz Marc's *The Mandrill*, discussed in the famous essay *On the Problem of Describing and Interpreting Works of the Visual*

67 *Ibid.*

68 Erwin Panofsky, 'Iconography and Iconology: An Introduction to the Study of Renaissance Art' (1939), in *Meaning in the Visual Arts: Papers in and on Art History* (Garden City, New York: Doubleday & C., 1955), pp. 26–54 (p. 29).

69 *Ibid.*, p. 30.

Arts[70], can still be regarded as an example of figurative art, given that a "trained" gaze can easily recognise a monkey in its natural habitat. On the contrary, *Vir Heroicus Sublimis* is a large-format canvas (approximately 2.5 metres tall and 5.4 metres wide) covered by a vast red field only broken by five vertical strips, and nothing else. So who is the *Vir* to whom the title refers? Where is the 'hero' of the painting? And why is he called 'sublime'? From Panofsky's perspective, these questions are of course utter nonsense: the polemical correspondence with Newman shows all the confusion and irritation of a person expecting to see men and heroes only to find nothing but a field of colour traversed by a few vertical lines (fig. 13).

Fig. 13 – Barnett Newman, *Vir Heroicus Sublimis* (1950–1951).
The Museum of Modern Art, New York.

And yet that *Vir* is indeed present, even if he is not represented. In order to find him (or rather, to make him manifest), we need to heed a piece of advice Newman offered on the occasion of his solo exhibition inaugurated on 23 April 1951 at the Betty Parsons

70 Erwin Panofsky, 'On the Problem of Describing and Interpreting Works of the Visual Arts' (1932), trans. by Jas Elsner and Katharina Lorenz, *Critical Inquiry*, 38, 3 (Spring 2012), 467–82.

Gallery in New York. On a sign hanging at the entrance to the room, visitors were presented with a short *vademecum* describing how best to view Newman's paintings: 'There is a tendency to look at large pictures from a distance. The large pictures in this exhibition are intended to be seen from a short distance'[71]. By following these enigmatic "instructions for use", inching ever closer to *Vir Heroicus Sublimis*, we suddenly find ourselves before the work, in its *presence*, overwhelmed by an immense sea of cadmium red. Almost drowning in colour, we instinctively cling to the zips as if to provide some sort of ballast. But these lines display no regularity, no geometrical disposition (so typical of Mondrian's compositions) that may help us reorient or steady ourselves; for here we are confronted with the absolute absence of rational measure.

The use of large canvases is characteristic of, but obviously not limited to, Abstract Expressionism: one need only think of the hundreds of huge pictures made during the Renaissance. Yet the *way* large canvases are used, as well as the *effects* they have on the beholder, are completely different. As Allan Kaprow argues, while Renaissance pictures 'glorified an idealized everyday world familiar to the observer, often continuing the actual room into the painting by means of *trompe l'œil*', abstract expressionist paintings offer no such familiarity; they in fact reverse the above procedure so that the painting is 'continued out into the room'[72]. In other words, a large-scale Renaissance picture still remains a *picture*: its essential function is depiction; its primary scope, beauty. Abstract Expressionism's way of using enormous canvases serves a different and even opposite purpose: the mural-scale paintings cease to be pictures – they become *environments*.

This, in turn, impacts on the beholder. Traditional pictures are meant as visual statements or symbolic representations: the viewer must "read" the meaning behind them. On the contrary, an abstract expressionist painting 'comes out at us'[73], forcing us to abandon the default attitude of detached contemplation, to

71 Newman, *Selected Writings and Interviews*, p. 178.

72 Allan Kaprow, 'The Legacy of Jackson Pollock', in *Essays on the Blurring of Art and Life*, ed. by Jeff Kelley (Berkeley–Los Angeles–London: University of California Press, 1993), pp. 1–9 (p. 6).

73 *Ibid.*

lose ourselves in the environment created by the artwork. To *lose* ourselves: because the transition from pictures to environmental paintings results in our being 'confronted, assaulted, sucked in'[74]. We are participants rather than observers; we experience the artwork rather than simply enjoy it. It is not for nothing that Edmund Burke considered 'greatness of dimensions' one of the most powerful causes of the sublime[75].

Moreover, the large-scale canvas of *Vir Heroicus Sublimis* is explicitly intended to be observed from up close, a feature common to many other abstract expressionist works of the time. Mark Rothko, for instance, requires his paintings to be hanged 'so that they must be first encountered at close quarters, so that the first experience is to be within the picture'[76]. Reflecting on the reasons behind such a request and on the effect this seemingly unnatural way of exhibiting large paintings has on the beholder, Michel Butor points out: 'You will have to stand so close to the canvas that you will lose sight of its general form, its frame; you will be steeped in this color, the margin appearing all around you as a horizon, the other masses of colour being presences, threats, influences within this space'[77].

This brings us back to the problem of framing. 'Form' and 'frame' go hand in hand with 'picture', 'beauty', and all the other notions at the core of the artistic tradition that abstract expressionists aimed to subvert. Being the opposite of beauty, the sublime is also the opposite of form: it is the formless. To use an all-enveloping, massive canvas meant to be seen from up close is to make viewers lose sight of the picture's form – its finitude, its boundaries. To experience the sublime, that is, the boundless, one has to feel "enveloped" and overwhelmed by the painting: one has

---

74 *Ibid.*

75 Edmund Burke, *A Philosophical Enquiry into the Origin of our Ideas of the Sublime and Beautiful* (1757), ed. with an intro. and notes by Adam Phillips (New York: Oxford University Press, 1998), pp. 124–25.

76 Mark Rothko, 'Letter to Katharine Kuh' (25 September 1954), in *Writings on Art*, ed. and with an intro., annotations, and chronology by Miguel López-Remiro (New Haven–London: Yale University Press, 2006), pp. 99–100 (p. 99).

77 Michel Butor, 'The Mosques of New York, or: The Art of Mark Rothko' (1961), in *Inventory: Essays*, trans., ed. and with a foreword by Richard Howard (London: Cape 1968), pp. 260–77 (p. 262).

to experience it 'more in terms of [...] environment than in those usually associated with a picture hung upon a wall'[78].

Removing the frame is therefore crucial to transforming painting from the 'production of pictures' into the 'generation of environments':

> With time, the obvious reference of every line and even stroke to the framing verticals and horizontals of the picture had turned into a constricting habit, but it was only in the middle and late 1940s, and in New York, that the way out was discovered to lie in a surface so large that its enclosing edges would lay outside or only on periphery of the artist's field of vision as he worked.[79]

Abstract Expressionism's attempt to overcome the paradigm of beauty and aesthetic appreciation could not but result in discarding the frame as an essential part of that paradigm – the paradigm of representation. If all borders are 'tools for *mediating* between the internal space of representation, occupied by the pictorial statement, and the external space'[80]; if the frame, as a particular instantiation of the concept of border, keeps the image separated from anything that is non-image, thus defining what is framed 'as a meaningful world, as opposed to the outside the frame, which is simply the world experienced'[81]; then the frame disappears (*must* disappear) when the need for this twofold act of separation and mediation is no longer required, when the spatio-temporal (real) world of the beholder and the spatio-temporal ("unreal") world of the image mutually collapse into each other.

The process of un-framing occurs once the traditional way of equating picture to representation, and representation to depiction, is rejected. Moreover, this gradual but steady process of "erosion" of the frame reflects an equally gradual and steady change in terms of worldviews: 'Just as the style of the Renaissance with its decisive feature, the frame and the closed homocentric

78 Clement Greenberg, 'American Abstract Painting' (1955), in *The Collected Essays and Criticism*, III, pp. 217–35 (p. 232).
79 Clement Greenberg, '"American-Type" Painting' (1958), in *Art and Culture*, pp. 208–29 (p. 219).
80 Groupe μ, 'Sémiotique et rhétorique du cadre', p. 116 (emphasis added).
81 Stoichita, *The Self-Aware Image*, p. 67.

space created by it, was an expression of a specific world order, so the dismantling of perspective and the discarding of the frame corresponds to that dissolution of boundaries [*Entgrenzung*] in which even man does not find his place anymore'[82]. The frame defines the 'classical' concept of painting as a form of representation that establishes its own space as clearly separated from the space of everyday life, presenting this separation as given and natural – not constructed[83]. This is precisely what abstract expressionists sought to challenge: 'classical' beauty as the unique and seemingly eternal ideal of art. The frame acts as a scaffolding for such an ideal: it establishes the coordinates of form, measure, and composition; it provides orientation; it suggests finiteness, completeness, and comprehensiveness; it determines the distance at which pictures should be contemplated in order for them to be aesthetically enjoyable. In the balance between the framing and the framed, 'the Western spirit achieves "classical" harmony'[84].

Therefore, if 'frames both represent a fundamental ordering principle and establish that ordering principle with regard to the work'[85], dismantling the frame means undermining the very notion of classical art. In the absence of the frame, the process through which abstract expressionist paintings 'encode the link with the beholder and how they acquire status'[86] becomes the object of a completely new negotiation – a negotiation that takes place in an uncharted territory of art and aesthetics:

> The edge as signifier of the limit is as if neutralized; the eye is distracted or hypnotized, and iterates the limit virtually on the space outside the painting. Unstopped by the punctuation of the picture frame, this movement of the gaze induces a sensation of limitlessness, maybe even of vertigo, intentionally of the sublime. Framelessness [...] serves to raise and suspend the question of limitation. The framed painting, by contrast, happily answers

82 Zaloscer, 'Versuch einer Phänomenologie des Rahmens', p. 218.

83 See Jean-Claude Lebensztejn, 'Framing Classical Space', *Art Journal*, 47, 1 (Spring 1988), 37–41 (p. 38).

84 Zaloscer, 'Versuch einer Phänomenologie des Rahmens', p. 224.

85 Thomas P. Brockelman, *The Frame and the Mirror: On Collage and the Postmodern* (Evanston: Northwestern University Press, 2001), p. 27.

86 Richard Phelan, 'The Picture Frame in Question: American Art 1945–2000', in Wolf and Bernhart (eds), *Framing Borders*, pp. 159–75 (p. 168).

> this question of limitation: 'yes', it says, 'the limit is here, look, you can't miss it, and, see, it can procure pleasure, excitement, delight'. Without the frame, however, the viewer in the early 1950s was at a loss, or, after Derrida, 'at a lack'. The result is that the question of the limit is left open, pending, in the air: present as a form of tension.[87]

This tension is soothed by the chromatic veils of Rothko's works, but thrust more bluntly upon us in Newman's paintings, which expose us to a form of anxiety, disorientation, and *unsettlement*. Such an unsettlement is a *sine qua non* for experiencing the sublime. Abstract expressionists tear art out of its comfort zone – out of its frame – and ditch it in the realm of discomfort.

Kant thought of this sublime discomfort as inextricably linked to 'chaos', to the 'wildest and most irregular disorder and desolation'[88]. To be sure, these very same terms can be used to describe the situation that humankind endured during and after World War II. And it is certainly no coincidence that it was precisely in this period that the abstract expressionists felt compelled to establish a completely new form of art:

> We felt the moral crisis of a world in shambles, a world devastated by a great depression and a fierce world war, and it was impossible at that time to paint the kind of paintings that we were doing – flowers, reclining nudes, and people playing the cello. At the same time we could not move into the situation of a pure world of unorganized shapes and forms, or color relations, a world of sensation. And I would say that for some of us, this was our moral crisis in relation to what to paint. So that we actually began, so to speak, from scratch, as if painting were not only dead but had never existed.[89]

Abstract Expressionism is a requiem not only for classical *art*, but also for the classical *worldview*: it attests to disorientation but, at the same time, attempts to provide a *new* orientation. Now, any discussion of 'worldviews' in art history inevitably leads to a discussion of iconology, which brings us back to Panofsky.

87 *Ibid.*, p. 166.
88 Kant, *Critique of Judgement*, p. 77.
89 Newman, *Selected Writings and Interviews*, p. 287.

His correspondence with Newman could have given the father of modern iconology the opportunity to do what he had never dared, namely, to extend his approach to non-figurative art. If he had managed to prise himself away from merely grammatical issues and actually taken *Vir Heroicus Sublimis* seriously, Panofsky would have found himself confronted with a new declination of the centuries-old notion of the sublime. But we know he chose not to. Ultimately, he *could* not have done otherwise, given that his hermeneutic methodology lies entirely within the paradigm of representation and is therefore aimed at describing and interpreting *pictures*.

If only he had bothered to read Rosenblum's article from which the infamous caption was taken, the elderly Princeton professor would have found out that the young art critic was striving to apply iconology to abstract art. Even just the layout of the essay (which Beat Wyss rightly compares to that used for the *Mnemosyne Atlas* by Aby Warburg, who exerted unmatched influence on Panofsky's thought)[90] surprisingly pairs figurative pictures belonging to the Romantic tradition, such as James Ward's *Gordale Scar* and John Martin's *The Creation*, with non-figurative paintings by Still, Rothko, Pollock, and Newman. In short, Rosenblum was trying to show that some major exponents of Abstract Expressionism directly referred to the traditional concept of the sublime – and this was, indeed, *iconography*. But he was also seeking to demonstrate that these artists offered a new perspective on the sublime by focusing on the dramatic disorientation of contemporary man and on the attempt to find a new orientation, a new worldview – and this was, indeed, *iconology*.

When confronted with *Vir Heroicus Sublimis*, Rosenblum argues, one feels like Caspar David Friedrich's famous *Wanderer above the Sea of Fog* or *Monk by the Sea*, which have become paradigmatic examples of the attempt to give visual expression to that feeling which a long and consolidated tradition has called the 'sublime'. Except now *we* are the wanderers, *we* are the monks, and the sea is the painting itself: we are no longer led to empathise with the characters portrayed, pretending to step into their shoes, for we now *are* in their shoes. There is no longer any filter,

90 Wyss, *Ein Druckfehler*, p. 6 and p. 18.

mediation, frame, or distance between us and the boundless, overwhelming force that seems to be 'about to engulf' us, as Frank O'Hara observed when describing the work of Newman's friend and colleague, Jackson Pollock[91].

However, in focussing on the analogies between the romantic and the abstract sublime, Rosenblum seemed to lose sight of a crucial difference. Romantic painters were still bound to the mimetic paradigm of representation: they could only create *beautiful pictures* of sublime natural things, like waterfalls or volcanoes. On the contrary, abstract expressionists were looking for the sublime in itself: for the *experience* of the sublime, not merely its representation. Rather than depicting sublime things, they sought to find a way to create paintings capable of eliciting in the person "encountering" them the feeling of the sublime[92].

In this sense, the Kantian opposition between beauty and the sublime was purposeful to the theoretical project of Abstract Expressionism as an artistic "movement" aimed at completely denying the traditional idea of beauty as the intrinsic content of all works of art *qua* works of art. Form and composition (the latter being the exact term used by Panofsky to define Newman's art in the first letter published in *ARTnews*, which proves that he had completely misunderstood the meaning of *Vir Heroicus Sublimis*) must be replaced by the formless and the measureless: only these traits may allow the viewer to experience the sublime. *Vir Heroicus Sublimis* is not to be found *within* the work, but *outside* of it: *Vir* is us. It is anyone who gives themselves to Newman's creation, who *experiences* it, who accepts being overwhelmed by its unfathomable boundlessness and dares to face the spatial, emotional, and cognitive disorientation that after all characterises human existence *tout court*. These feelings were certainly strong in post-World War II America, but they are more generally characteristic of *homo duplex*, that is, of human beings as 'rational animals' essentially torn between sensibility and reason, instinct and intellect, impulse and reflection:

---

91 Frank O' Hara, *Jackson Pollock* (New York: Braziller, 1959), p. 29.
92 See on this Danto, 'Barnett Newman and the Heroic Sublime', p. 27.

> The present painter is concerned not with his own feelings or with the mystery of his own personality but with the penetration into the world-mystery. His imagination is therefore attempting to dig into metaphysical secrets. To that extent his art is concerned with the sublime. It is a religious art which through symbols will catch the basic truth of life, which is its sense of *tragedy*.[93]

Newman's canvases take on a (literally) 'enveloping and englobing'[94] dimension that turns a simple spectator into an authentic, albeit involuntary, actor. They invite us not to contemplate the work with quiet and detached aesthetic attitude, but rather to become part of the work itself, to lose ourselves in it as if in a new and unknown world that leaves us defenceless. We must move closer to the painting if we are to experience its violence, to be in its thrall. The disorientation generated by the absence of any mimetic form, of any reassuring measure or regularity, is only the first step toward understanding, or rather *activating* the 'artwork' – making the art *work*, so to speak.

The second step, complementary to the first, transforms a seemingly negative experience into a properly sublime experience, which always entails an oxymoronic coexistence of pleasure and displeasure. Kant described the experience of the sublime as unfolding in two stages. First, it implies an 'excess for the imagination', like 'an abyss in which it fears to lose itself'. Secondly, it presupposes that what is excessive for one's sensibility and imagination can instead be embraced by the faculty of reason and 'the rational idea of the supersensible'[95]. Indeed, this is precisely what Newman and the abstract expressionists were looking for – the supersensible: 'The European [painter] is concerned with the transcendence of objects while the American is concerned with the reality of the transcendental experience'[96]. The idea and even

93 Newman, 'The Plasmic Image', p. 140 (emphasis added).

94 Michele Bertolini, 'Dall'astratto sublime allo stile trascendentale: il luogo dello spettatore fra distanza ed empatia in alcuni momenti dell'esperienza estetica contemporanea', in *Estetica della fruizione. Sentimento, giudizio di gusto e piacere estetico*, ed. by Maddalena Mazzocut-Mis (Milan: Lupetti, 2008), pp. 385–424 (p. 394).

95 Kant, *Critique of Judgement*, p. 88.

96 Barnett Newman, 'Response to Clement Greenberg' (1947), in *Selected Writings and Interviews*, pp. 161–64 (p. 164).

the words Newman uses directly refer to Kant's explanation of the sublime as an experience of boundlessness and framelessness:

> We have no reason to fear that the feeling of the sublime will suffer from an abstract mode of presentation [...], which is altogether negative with regard to the sensuous. For though the imagination, no doubt, finds nothing beyond the sensible world on which it can lay hold, still this thrusting aside of the sensible barriers gives it a feeling of being *unbounded*; and that removal is thus a presentation of the infinite [*eine Darstellung des Unendlichen*]. As such it can never be anything more than a negative presentation – but still it expands the soul. Perhaps there is no more sublime passage in the Jewish Law than the commandment: Thou shalt not make unto thee any graven image, or any likeness of any thing that is in heaven or on earth, or under the earth, etc.[97]

We can now understand Arthur Danto's statement that 'it was as though Newman had hit upon a way of being a painter without violating the Second Commandment, which prohibits images'[98]: his paintings do not *represent* anything, they rather *present* themselves, and that is it. As Jean-François Lyotard argued, *Vir Heroicus Sublimis* 'belongs to the Annunciations, the Epiphanies'[99]. It is a sort of evangelical message, even if 'the message "speaks" of nothing; it emanates from no one. It is not Newman who is speaking, or who is using painting to show us something. The message (the painting) is the messenger; it "says": 'Here I am', in other words, 'I am yours' or 'Be mine'. [...] The message is the presentation, but it presents nothing; it is, that is, presence'[100].

Revelation is the manifestation of something that was either not there before or not necessary at all – and yet it *is* indeed there. Newman's paintings seem easy to describe, but the description is 'as flat as a paraphrase. The best gloss consists of the question: what can one say? Or of the exclamation "Ah". Of surprise: "Look

97 Kant, *Critique of Judgement*, p. 88 (emphasis added).
98 Danto, 'Barnett Newman and the Heroic Sublime', p. 27.
99 Jean-François Lyotard, 'Newman: The Instant' (1984), in *The Inhuman: Reflections on Time*, trans. by Geoffrey Bennington and Rachel Bowlby (Cambridge: Polity Press, 1991), pp. 78–88 (p. 79).
100 *Ibid.*, p. 81.

at that". So many expressions of a feeling which does have a name in the modern aesthetic tradition (and in the work of Newman): the sublime. It is feeling of "there [*voilà*]"'[101]. This 'there' is not merely the artwork intended as a physical object, but rather the event that manifests *through*, and *thanks to*, the artwork. It is the feeling that binds the viewer to the work, the feeling of the indescribable, unutterable presence of the event: 'One would have to read *The Sublime Is Now* not as *The Sublime Is Now* but as *Now the Sublime Is Like This*. Not elsewhere, not up there or over there, not earlier or later, not once upon a time. But as here, now, it happens that... and it's this painting. Here and now there is this painting, rather than nothing, and that's what is sublime'[102]. Lyotard's interpretation is perfectly in line with Newman's way of explaining his own work as a painter:

> One thing that I am involved in about painting is that the painting should give man a sense of place: that he knows he's there, so he's aware of himself. In that sense he relates to me when I made the painting because in that sense I was there. [...] This is what I have tried to do: that the onlooker in front of my painting knows that he is there. To me, the sense of place not only has a mystery but has that sense of metaphysical fact.[103]

This, in the end, is *Vir Heroicus Sublimis*: an *encounter* between the painting and the experiencer, an event in which both come to be present in the very same space and at the very same time: 'It's no different, really, from one's feeling a relation to meeting another person'[104]. Encountering a painting "in person" means dramatically altering the traditional aesthetic enjoyment as characterised by image consciousness, distance, mediateness, and the separation between the artwork and the beholder. The frame embodies and epitomises all of these aspects of aesthetic experience. In order to subvert the paradigm of 'classical' beauty and to replace it with a new, sublime worldview, abstract expressionists had to find a

101 *Ibid.*, p. 80.
102 Jean-François Lyotard, 'The Sublime and the Avant-Garde' (1984), in *The Inhuman*, pp. 89–107 (p. 93).
103 Barnett Newman, 'Interview with David Sylvester', p. 257.
104 *Ibid.*, p. 259.

way to put their artworks *in touch* with the beholder without the assistance of any mediation: they had to de-isolate art, discarding the frame and, with it, the whole dispositif of representation. And that is exactly what they did.

One last observation must be made concerning frames in Abstract Expressionism. Even though there is no parergonal closure in Newman, Rothko, or Pollock, they all intended for their works to be presented within the secular temple of the museum, that is, again, within a cultural, institutional *frame*[105]. The walls on which paintings are hung, the rooms in which they are exhibited, the art criticism that classifies them as artworks: all of these variables constitute, indeed, different kinds of framing. To remove even this last frame, the artwork itself has to be removed from the museum or from whatever conventional cultural venue in which it is housed. After Abstract Expressionism, the next step towards the transformation of pictures into environments is to completely merge the artwork with its surroundings: in this sense, land art seems to have brought the process of unframing to its natural conclusion. Unless, of course, we choose to consider the whole world as a boundless, endless – and therefore, paradoxically, frameless – frame.

105 See on this Anne Temkin (ed.), *Barnett Newman* (Philadelphia: Museum of Art, 2002), p. 64; and Phelan, 'The Picture Frame in Question', p. 174.

REFERENCES

Abell, Catharine, and Katerina Bantinaki (eds), *Philosophical Perspectives on Depiction* (Oxford–New York: Oxford University Press, 2010).

Alberti, Leon Battista, *On Painting: A New Translation and Critical Edition*, ed. and trans. by Rocco Sinisgalli (Cambridge: Cambridge University Press, 2011).

Arasse, Daniel, *Histoires de peintures* (Paris: France Culture–Denoël, 2004).

Archambault de Beaune, Sophie, 'Chamanisme et préhistoire : Un feuilleton à épisodes', *L'Homme*, 147 (1998), 203–19.

Aretino, Pietro, *Lettere sull'Arte*, ed. by Ettore Camesasca, 2 vols (Milan: Edizioni del Milione, 1957), II, pp. 16–18.

Arnheim, Rudolf, 'The Robin and the Saint: On the Twofold Nature of the Artistic Image', *The Journal of Aesthetics and Art Criticism*, 18, 1 (1959), 68–79.

– *Art and Visual Perception: A Psychology of the Creative Eye*, expanded and revised edition (Berkeley–Los Angeles–London: University of California Press, 1974).

– 'Limits and Frames', in *The Power of the Center: A Study of Composition in the Visual Arts* (Berkeley: University of California Press, 1982), pp. 42–70.

Aumont, Jacques, *L'œil interminable. Cinema et peinture* (Toulose: Seguier, 1989).

Bach, Ferdinand-Sigismond, *Le voyage à Berlin : La fin de l'Allemagne romantique* (Paris: Conard, 1929).

Bal, Mieke, *Reading Art*, in *Generations and Geographies in the Visual Arts: Feminist Readings*, ed. by Griselda Pollock (London: Routledge, 1996), pp. 25–41.

– *Travelling Concepts in the Humanities: A Rough Guide* (Toronto: University of Toronto Press, 2002).

Baudrillard, Jean, *The Perfect Crime* (1995), trans. by Chris Turner (London–New York: Verso, 2002).

Bégout, Bruce, 'Duane Hanson grandeur nature', in *Duane Hanson. Le Rêve américain…* (Paris: Actes Sud–Parc de la Villette, 2010), pp. 7–12.
Benjamin, Walter, *The Arcades Project*, trans. by Howard Eiland and Kevin McLaughlin (Cambridge MA–London: Belknap Press, 1999).
Berrouet, Florian, 'La part du corps : chamanisme et écriture', *Communication & Langages*, 186, 4 (2015), 5–25.
Bertolini, Michele, 'Dall'astratto sublime allo stile trascendentale: il luogo dello spettatore fra distanza ed empatia in alcuni momenti dell'esperienza estetica contemporanea', in *Estetica della fruizione. Sentimento, giudizio di gusto e piacere estetico*, ed. by Maddalena Mazzocut-Mis (Milan: Lupetti, 2008), pp. 385–424.
Blumenberg, Hans, *Höhlenausgänge* (Frankfurt a.M.: Suhrkamp, 1989).
Bois, Yve-Alain, '"The Wild" and Company', *October*, 143 (2013), 95–125.
Bolter, Jay David, and Richard Grusin, *Remediation: Understanding New Media* (Cambridge MA–London: The MIT Press, 1999).
Breton, André, *Nadja* (1928), trans. by Richard Howard (New York: Grove Press, 1960).
Brockelman, Thomas P., *The Frame and the Mirror: On Collage and the Postmodern* (Evanston: Northwestern University Press, 2001).
Buchsteiner, Thomas, 'Art Is Life, and Life Is Realistic', in *Duane Hanson: More than Reality*, ed. by Thomas Buchsteiner and Otto Letze, (Ostfildern: Hatje Cantz, 2007), pp. 68–79.
Burke, Edmund, *A Philosophical Enquiry into the Origin of our Ideas of the Sublime and Beautiful* (1757), ed. with an intro. and notes by Adam Phillips (New York: Oxford University Press, 1998).
Burkert, Walter, *Structure and History in Greek Mythology and Ritual* (Berkeley–Los Angeles–London: University of California Press, 1979).
Bush, Martin H. (ed.), *Sculptures by Duane Hanson* (Wichita: Wichita State University, 1985).
Butler, Samuel, *Alps and Sanctuaries of Piedmont and the Canton Ticino* (London: Bogue, 1881).
Butor, Michel, 'The Mosques of New York, or: The Art of Mark Rothko' (1961), in *Inventory: Essays*, trans., ed. and with a foreword by Richard Howard (London: Cape, 1968), pp. 260–77.
Calì, Carmelo, *Husserl e l'immagine* (Palermo: Aesthetica, 2002).
Calleja, Gordon, *In-Game: From Immersion to Incorporation* (Cambridge MA–London: The MIT Press, 2011).
Carbone, Mauro, 'Thematizing the "Arche-Screen" through Its Variations', trans. by Marta Nijhuis, in *Screens: From Materiality to Spectatorship – A Historical and Theoretical Reassessment*, ed. by Dominique Chateau and José Moure (Amsterdam: Amsterdam University Press, 2016), pp. 62–69.

Charbonnier, Louise, *Cadre et regard.* Généalogie d'un dispositif, preface by Jean-Claude Soulages (Paris: L'Harmattan, 2007).

Charlesworth, J.J., 'Is Duane Hanson's Sentimentality for Working People Noble or Just Patronizing?', *Artnet News*, 9 June 2015.

Chesterton, Gilbert K., 'The Toy Theatre', in *Tremendous Trifles* (1909) (Mineola–New York: Dover, 2012), pp. 176-84.

Clottes, Jean, and David Lewis-Williams, *Les chamanes de la Préhistoire. Transe et magie dans les grottes ornées* (Paris: Le Seuil, 1996).

Coleridge, Samuel Taylor, *Biographia Literaria* (1817), ed. by James Engel and Walter Jackson Bate, 2 vols (Princeton: Princeton University Press, 1985).

Conte, Pietro, *In carne e cera. Estetica e fenomenologia dell'iperrealismo* (Macerata: Quodlibet, 2014).

Crowther, Paul, *Phenomenology of the Visual Arts (Even the Frame)* (Stanford: Stanford University Press, 2009).

Danto, Arthur C., 'Barnett Newman and the Heroic Sublime', The Nation, 16 June 2002, 25–29.

Därmann, Iris, *Tod und Bild. Eine phänomenologische Mediengeschichte* (Munich: Fink, 1995).

Daston, Lorraine, and Peter Galison, *Objectivity* (New York: Zone Books, 2007).

Dembeck, Till, *Texte rahmen. Grenzregionen literarischer Werke im 18. Jahrhundert* (Berlin–New York: de Gruyter, 2007).

Dennett, Daniel C., 'Where am I?', in Douglas R. Hofstadter and Daniel C. Dennett, *The Mind's I: Fantasies and Reflections on Mind and Soul* (New York: Basic Books, 1981), pp. 217–29.

Derrida, Jacques, *The Truth in Painting* (1978), trans. by Geoffrey Bennington and Ian McLeod (Chicago–London: The University of Chicago Press, 1987).

Diderot, Denis, *Salon 1763*, ed. by Jean Seznec and Jean Adhémar, 4 vols (Oxford: Clarendon Press, 1975).

Dissanayake, Ellen, *Homo Aestheticus: Where Art Comes from and Why* (Seattle–London: University of Washington Press, 1995).

Du Bos, Jean-Baptiste, *Critical Reflections on Poetry, Painting, and Music* (1719), trans. by Thomas Nugent (New York: AMS, 1978).

Dubois, Philippe, *L'acte photographique* (Bruxelles: Labor, 1983).

Duro, Paul (ed.), *The Rhetoric of the Frame: Essays on the Boundaries of the Artwork* (Cambridge: Cambridge University Press, 1996).

Eisenstein, Sergei, 'On Stereocinema' (1947), trans. by Sergey Levchin, in *3D Cinema and Beyond*, ed. by Dan Adler, Janine Marchessault, and Sanja Obradovic (Bristol: Intellect, 2013), pp. 20–59.

Fimiani, Filippo, 'Une esthétique imperceptible', *Figures de l'art*, 1 (2009), 217–37.

Fink, Eugen, 'Vergegenwärtigung und Bild. Beiträge zur Phänomenologie der Unwirklichkeit', *Jahrbuch für Philosophie und phänomenologische Forschung*, 11 (1930), 239–309.
Frankfurter, Alfred, 'Letter to E. Panofsky' (9 August 1961), in Panofsky, *Korrespondenz 1957 bis 1961*, p. 1003.
Freedberg, David, *The Power of Images: Studies in the History and Theory of Response* (Chicago: The University of Chicago Press, 1989).
Geiger, Moritz, 'Beiträge zur Phänomenologie des ästhetischen Genusses', *Jahrbuch für Philosophie und Phänomenologische Forschung*, 1 (1913), 567–684.
Ghiron, Valeria, *La teoria dell'immaginazione di Edmund Husserl: fantasia e coscienza figurale nella "fenomenologia descrittiva"* (Venice: Marsilio, 2001).
Ghirri, Luigi, *Il profilo delle nuvole. Immagini di un paesaggio italiano*, texts by Gianni Celati (Milan: Feltrinelli, 1989).
– *Lezioni di fotografia*, ed. by Giulio Bizzarri and Paolo Barbaro, with a biographical text by Gianni Celati (Macerata: Quodlibet, 2010).
Gilbert, Annette, 'Leere Rahmen. Das Unsichtbare des Sichtbaren sichtbar machen', in *Rahmenbrüche, Rahmenwechsel*, ed. by Uwe Wirth in collaboration with Julia Paganini (Berlin: Kadmos, 2013), pp. 217–37.
Gombrich, Ernst, 'Meditations on a Hobby Horse or the Roots of Artistic Form' (1951), in *Meditations on a Hobby Horse and Other Essays on the Theory of Art* (Oxford: Phaidon, 1963), pp. 1–11.
– *Art and Illusion: A Study in the Psychology of Pictorial Representation* (1960) (Princeton–Oxford: Princeton University Press, 2000).
Grande, John K., 'Americanacirema', *Espace: Art actuel*, 28 (1994), 19–22.
Grau, Oliver, *Virtual Art: From Illusion to Immersion* (Cambridge MA–London: The MIT Press, 2003).
Greenberg, Clement, 'Seurat, Science, and Art: Review of *Georges Seurat* by John Rewald' (1943), in *The Collected Essays and Criticism*, I, pp. 167–70.
– 'The Crisis of the Easel Picture' (1948), in *The Collected Essays and Criticism*, II, pp. 221–25.
– 'Kandinsky' (1948, 1957), in *Art and Culture*, pp. 111–14.
– 'Contribution to a Symposium' (1953), in *Art and Culture*, pp. 124–26.
– 'Abstract and Representational' (1954), in *The Collected Essays and Criticism*, III, pp. 186–93.
– 'American Abstract Painting' (1955), in *The Collected Essays and Criticism*, III, pp. 217–35.
– '"American-Type" Painting' (1958), in *Art and Culture*, pp. 208–29.
– 'The Later Monet' (1959), in *Art and Culture*, pp. 37–45.
– *Art and Culture: Critical Essays* (Boston: Beacon Press, 1961).

– *The Collected Essays and Criticism*, ed. by John O'Brian, 4 vols (Chicago–London: The University of Chicago Press, 1986).

Gregg, Ryan, 'The Sacro Monte of Varallo as a Physical Manifestation of the Spiritual Exercises', *Athanor*, 22 (2004), 49–55.

Groupe µ, 'Sémiotique et rhétorique du cadre', *La part de l'œil*, 5 (1989), 115–31.

Harries, Karsten, *The Broken Frame: Three Lectures* (Washington, DC: Catholic University of America Press, 1989).

Halwani, Miriam (ed.), *Karl Schenker's Mondäne Bildwelten* (Köln: König, 2016).

Hegel, Georg Wilhelm Friedrich, *Aesthetics: Lectures on Fine Art*, trans. by Thomas Malcolm Knox, 2 vols (Oxford: Oxford University Press, 1975).

Houser, Kristin, 'Neuroreality: The New Reality Is Coming. And It's a Brain Computer Interface', *Futurism*, 26 July 2017.

Huhtamo, Erkki, *Illusions in Motion: Media Archaeology of the Moving Panorama and Related Spectacles* (Cambridge MA–London: The MIT Press, 2013).

Husserl, Edmund, 'Phantasy and Image Presentation' (1898), in *Phantasy, Image Consciousness, and Memory (1898–1925)*, pp. 117–51.

– *Logical Investigations* (1900–1901), trans. by John N. Findlay, ed. by Dermot Moran, 2 vols (London–New York: Routledge, 2001).

– 'Phantasy and Image Consciousness' (1904–1905), in *Phantasy, Image Consciousness, and Memory (1898–1925)*, pp. 1–115.

– 'Vitality and Suitability in Re-Presentation; Empty Re-Presentation. Internal Consciousness, Internal Reflection. The Strict Concept of Reproduction' (1911–1912), in *Phantasy, Image Consciousness, and Memory (1898–1925)*, pp. 363–74.

– 'Modes of Reproduction and Phantasy Image Consciousness' (1912), in *Phantasy, Image Consciousness, and Memory (1898–1925)*, pp. 401–82.

– 'On the Analysis of Memory. Characterization of Internal Memory and Characterization through the Later Nexus: Omission and Supervention of Position Takings' (1912), in *Phantasy, Image Consciousness, and Memory*, pp. 497–507.

– 'On the Theory of Image Consciousness and Figment Consciousness' (1912), in *Phantasy, Image Consciousness, and Memory*, pp. 581–99.

– 'Reproduction and Image Consciousness', Appendix L: 'On Imagination' (1912), in *Phantasy, Image Consciousness, and Memory*, pp. 569–73.

– 'On the Theory of Intuitions and Their Modes' (1918), in *Phantasy, Image Consciousness, and Memory*, pp. 599–658.

– *Phantasy, Image Consciousness, and Memory (1898–1925)*, trans. by John B. Brough (Dordrecht: Springer, 2005).

– *Experience and Judgment: Investigations in a Genealogy of Logic* (1948), trans. by James Spencer Churchill and Karl Ameriks, ed. by Ludwig Landgrebe (Evanston: Northwestern University Press, 1973).

Husson, Jules-François-Félix (Champfleury), *Les excentriques* (Paris: Michel Lévy Frères, 1855).

Janson, Horst Waldemar, 'After Betsy, What?', *Bulletin of the Atomic Scientists*, 15, 2 (1959), 68–71 and 93.

Jirsa, Tomáš, 'Lost in Pattern: Rococo Ornament and Its Journey to Contemporary Art through Wallpaper', in *Where Is History Today? New Ways of Representing the Past*, ed. by Marcel Arbeit and Ian Christie (Olomouc: Palacký University, 2015), pp. 101–19.

Kaell, Hillary, *Walking Where Jesus Walked: American Christians and Holy Land Pilgrimage* (New York: New York University Press, 2014).

Kande, Sylvie, 'Note de lecture', *Autrepart. Revue de sciences sociales au Sud*, 67–68 (2013), 281–83.

Kant, Immanuel, *Critique of Judgement* (1790), trans. by James Creed Meredith, ed. by Nicholas Walker (Oxford: Oxford University Press, 2007).

Kaprow, Allan, 'The Legacy of Jackson Pollock', in *Essays on the Blurring of Art and Life*, ed. by Jeff Kelley (Berkeley–Los Angeles–London: University of California Press, 1993), pp. 1–9.

Klammer, Markus, 'Kommentar zu *Der Rahmen der Repräsentation und einige seiner Figuren* von Louis Marin', *Zeitschrift für Medien- und Kulturforschung*, 7, 1 (2016), 99–108.

Koolhaas, Rem, *Delirious New York: A Retroactive Manifesto for Manhattan* (New York: Oxford University Press, 1978).

Körner, Hans, and Karl Möseneder (eds), *Rahmen – Zwischen Innen und Außen: Beiträge zur Theorie und Geschichte* (Berlin: Reimer, 2010).

Kubler, George, 'Disjunction and Mutational Energy', *ARTnews*, 60, 1 (1961), 34 and 55.

– 'Sacred Mountains in Europe and America', in *Christianity and the Renaissance: Image and Religious Imagination in the Quattrocento*, ed. by Timothy G. Verdon and John Henderson (Syracuse: Syracuse University Press, 1990), pp. 413–41.

Lange, Konrad, *Die künstlerische Erziehung der deutschen Jugend* (Darmstadt: Bergsträsser, 1893).

– *Die bewusste Selbsttäuschung als Kern des künstlerischen Genusses* (Leipzig: Veit, 1895).

– *Das Wesen der Kunst. Grundzüge einer realistischen Kunstlehre*, 2 vols (Berlin: Grote'sche Verlagsbuchhandlung, 1904).

– *Das Wesen der Kunst. Grundzüge einer illusionistischen Kunstlehre* (Berlin: Grote'sche Verlagsbuchhandlung, 1907).

Lauzon, Jean, *La photographie malgré l'image* (Ottawa: Presses de l'Université d'Ottawa, 2002).
Lebensztejn, Jean-Claude, 'A partir du cadre (vignettes)' (1987), in *Annexes – de l'oeuvre d'art* (Paris: La Part de l'Œil, 1999), pp. 181–223.
– 'Framing Classical Space', *Art Journal*, 47, 1 (Spring 1988), 37–41.
Lenain, Thierry, *La peinture des singes. Histoire et esthétique*, pref. by Desmond Morris (Paris: Syros–Alternatives, 1990).
Lenain, Thierry, and Rudy Steinmetz (eds), *Cadre, seuil, limite. La question de la frontière dans la théorie de l'art* (Bruxelles: La lettre volée, 2010).
Liptay, Fabienne, and Burcu Dogramaci (eds), *Immersion in the Visual Arts and Media* (Leiden–Boston: Brill Rodopi, 2016).
Long, Burke O., *Imagining the Holy Land: Maps, Models, and Fantasy Travels* (Bloomington: Indiana University Press, 2003).
Lyotard, Jean-François, 'Newman: The Instant' (1984), in *The Inhuman: Reflections on Time*, trans. by Geoffrey Bennington and Rachel Bowlby (Cambridge: Polity Press, 1991), pp. 78–88.
– 'The Sublime and the Avant-Garde' (1984), in *The Inhuman: Reflections on Time*, trans. by Geoffrey Bennington and Rachel Bowlby (Cambridge: Polity Press, 1991), pp. 89–107.
Marbach, Eduard, *Mental Representation and Consciousness: Toward a Phenomenological Theory of Representation and Reference* (Dordrecht–Boston–London: Kluwer, 1993).
Marcus, Hugo, 'Rahmen, Formenschönheit und Bildinneres', *Zeitschrift für Ästhetik und allgemeine Kunstwissenschaft*, 8 (1913), 73–93.
Marin, Louis, 'Les combles et les marges de la représentation', *Rivista di estetica*, 25 (1984), 11–33.
– 'Figures of Reception in Modern Representation in Painting' (1985), trans. by Catherine Porter, in *On Representation*, pp. 320–36.
– 'The Frame of Representation and Some of Its Figures' (1988), in *On Representation*, pp. 352–72.
– *On Representation*, trans. by Catherine Porter (Stanford: Stanford University Press, 2001).
Martins, José Manuel, '"Crows" vs "Avatar": or, 3D vs Total-Dimension Immersion', *Film and Media Studies*, 8 (2014), 79–96.
Mendelssohn, Moses, 'On the Main Principles of the Fine Arts and Sciences' (1757), in *Philosophical Writings*, trans. and ed. by Daniel O. Dahlstrom (Cambridge: Cambridge University Press, 1997), pp. 169–91.
Merleau-Ponty, Maurice, *Phenomenology of Perception* (1945), trans. by Colin Smith (London–New York: Routledge, 2013).
Meschiari, Matteo, 'Sciamanesimo paleolitico europeo. Paradigmi ermeneutici e riesame fenomenologico dell'arte parietale franco-

cantabrica', in *Le origini sciamaniche della cultura europea*, ed. by Francesco Benozzo (Alessandria: Edizioni dell'Orso, 2015), pp. 21–54.
Moritz, Karl Philipp, 'Zufälligkeit und Bildung vom Isoliren in Rücksicht auf die schönen Künste überhaupt' (1789), in *Schriften zur Aesthetik und Poetik*, ed. by Hans Joachim Schrimpf (Tübingen: Max Niemeyer, 1962), pp. 116–17.
– *Vorbegriffe zu einer Theorie der Ornamente* (Berlin: Karl Massdorff, 1793).
Morris, Desmond, *The Biology of Art: A Study of the Picture-Making Behaviour of the Great Apes and Its Relationship to Human Art* (London: Methuen, 1962).
Müller, Claudia, *Beobachtungen am und über den Rand hinaus* (Hamburg: Hochschule für bildende Künste Hamburg, 2007).
Newman, Barnett, 'The Plasmic Image' (1945), in *Selected Writings and Interviews*, pp. 138–55.
– 'Teresa Zarnower' (1946), in *Selected Writings and Interviews*, pp. 103–05.
– 'Response to Clement Greenberg' (1947), in *Selected Writings and Interviews*, pp. 161–64.
– 'The Sublime Is Now' (1948), in *Selected Writings and Interviews*, pp. 170–73.
– 'Letter to the Editor of The New York Times Magazine' (7 June 1954), in *Selected Writings and Interviews*, pp. 40–41.
– 'Letter to A. Frankfurter', *ARTnews*, 60, 3 (May 1961), 6. Reprinted in Panofsky, *Korrespondenz 1957 bis 1961*, pp. 931–32.
– 'Letter to A. Frankfurter', *ARTnews*, 60, 5 (September 1961), 6. Reprinted in Panofsky, *Korrespondenz 1957 bis 1961*, pp. 1016–19, as well as in Newman, *Selected Writings and Interviews*, pp. 219–20.
– 'Interview with Lane Slate' (1963), in *Selected Writings and Interviews*, pp. 251–54.
– 'Interview with David Sylvester' (1965), in *Selected Writings and Interviews*, pp. 254–59.
– 'A Conversation: Barnett Newman and Thomas Hess' (1966), in *Selected Writings and Interviews*, pp. 273–86.
– 'Interview with Emile de Antonio' (1970), in *Selected Writings and Interviews*, pp. 302–08.
– *Selected Writings and Interviews*, ed. by John P. O'Neill, text notes and commentary by Mollie McNickle, intro. by Richard Shiff (Berkeley–Los Angeles: University of California Press, 1992).
Nova, Alessandro, 'Popular Art in Renaissance Italy: Early Response to the Holy Mountain at Varallo', in *Reframing the Renaissance: Visual*

Culture in Europe and Latin America, 1450–1650, ed. by Claire J. Farago (New Haven–London: Yale University Press, 1995), pp. 113–26.

O' Hara, Frank, *Jackson Pollock* (New York: Braziller, 1959).

O'Doherty, Brian, *Inside the White Cube: The Ideology of the Gallery Space*, Expanded Edition (Berkeley–Los Angeles: University of California Press, 1999).

Oettermann, Stephan, *Das Panorama: Die Geschichte eines Massenmediums* (Frankfurt a.M.: Syndikat, 1980).

Ortega y Gasset, José, 'Meditations on the Frame' (1921), trans. by Andrea L. Bell, *Perspecta*, 26 (1990), 185–90.

Panofsky, Erwin, 'On the Problem of Describing and Interpreting Works of the Visual Arts' (1932), trans. by Jas Elsner and Katharina Lorenz, *Critical Inquiry*, 38, 3 (Spring 2012), 467–82.

– 'Iconography and Iconology: An Introduction to the Study of Renaissance Art' (1939), in *Meaning in the Visual Arts: Papers in and on Art History* (Garden City, New York: Doubleday & C., 1955), pp. 26–54.

– 'Letter to W.S. Heckscher', 22 April 1957, in *Korrespondenz 1957 bis 1961*, pp. 95–96.

– 'Letter to G. Kepes' (11 November 1958), in Panofsky, *Korrespondenz 1957 bis 1961*, pp. 357–58.

– 'Letter to W.H. Woody Jr.' (14 November 1958), in *Korrespondenz 1957 bis 1961*, pp. 358–62.

– 'Letter to J. Canaday' (17 September 1959), in *Korrespondenz 1957 bis 1961*, pp. 526–28.

– *Renaissance and Renascences in Western Art* (1960) (New York: Harper & Row, 1972).

– 'Letter to H.A. La Farge' (20 February 1961), *ARTnews*, 60, 2 (April), 6. Reprinted in Erwin Panofsky, *Korrespondenz 1957 bis 1961*, ed. by Dieter Wuttke (Wiesbaden: Harrassowitz, 2008), pp. 872–73.

– 'Letter to A. Frankfurter' (18 August 1961), in *Korrespondenz 1957 bis 1961*, p. 1010.

– 'Letter to A. Frankfurter', *ARTnews*, 60, 5 (September 1961), 6. Reprinted in Panofsky, *Korrespondenz 1957 bis 1961*, pp. 956–57.

- *Korrespondenz 1957 bis 1961*, ed. by Dieter Wuttke (Wiesbaden: Harrassowitz, 2008).

Phelan, Richard, 'The Picture Frame in Question: American Art 1945–2000', in Wolf and Bernhart (eds), *Framing Borders*, pp. 159–75.

Philippot, Paul, 'Restoration from the Perspective of the Humanities', in *Historical and Philosophical Issues in the Conservation of Cultural Heritage*, ed. by Nicholas Stanley Price, Mansfield Kirby Talley, and Alessandra Melucco Vaccaro (Los Angeles: Getty Conservation Institute, 1996), pp. 216–29.

Piana, Giovanni, *Elementi di una dottrina dell'esperienza. Saggio di filosofia fenomenologica* (1979) (Milan: Cuem, 2005).

Pinhanez, Claudio, and Mark Podlaseck, 'To Frame or Not to Frame: The Role and Design of Frameless Displays in Ubiquitous Applications', in *Ubiquitous Computing. Lecture Notes in Computer Science*, vol. 3660, ed. by Michael Beigl *et al.* (Berlin–Heidelberg: Springer, 2005). https://doi.org/10.1007/11551201_20.

Pinotti, Andrea (ed.), *Estetica ed empatia* (Milan: Guerini, 1997).

– 'The Painter through the Fourth Wall of China: Benjamin and the Threshold of the Image', in *Benjamin-Studien 3*, ed. by Sigrid Weigel and Daniel Weidner (Munich: Fink, 2014), pp. 133–49.

– 'Self-Negating Images: Towards An-Iconology', *Proceedings*, 1 (2017), 1–9 (doi:10.3390/proceedings1090856).

– 'La cornice come oggetto teorico', in *La cornice. Storie, teorie, testi*, ed. by Daniela Ferrari and Andrea Pinotti (Milan: Johan & Levi, 2018), pp. 51–67.

– 'Environmentalising the Image: Towards An-Iconology', *Screen*, 2020.

Poussin, Nicolas, 'Correspondance', ed. by Charles Jouanny, *Archives de l'Art français, Nouvelle période*, 5 (1968).

Putnam, Hilary, 'Brains in a Vat', in *Reason, Truth and History* (Cambridge: Cambridge University Press, 1981), pp. 1–21.

Quatremère de Quincy, Antoine Chrysostome, *An Essay on the Nature, the End, and the Means of Imitation in the Fine Arts* (1823), trans. by J. C. Kent (London: Smith, Elder & co., 1837).

Ranke, Leopold von, *Geschichten der romanischen und germanischen Völker von 1494 bis 1514* (1824), in *Leopold von Rankes Sämmtliche Werke*, 54 vols (Leipzig: Duncker & Humblot, 1867–1890), XXXIII (1874).

Rosenblum, Robert, 'The Abstract Sublime', *ARTnews*, 60, 1 (February 1961), 39–40 and 56–58.

Rothko, Mark, 'Letter to Katharine Kuh' (25 September 1954), in *Writings on Art*, ed. and with an intro., annotations, and chronology by Miguel López-Remiro (New Haven–London: Yale University Press, 2006), pp. 99–100.

– 'Interview with Dorothy Seiberling', Life, 16 November 1959, p. 82.

Schapiro, Meyer, 'On Some Problems in the Semiotics of Visual Arts: Field and Vehicle in Image-Signs', *Simiolus: Netherlands Quarterly for the History of Art*, 6, 1 (1972–1973), 9–19.

Schlosser, Julius von, 'Dialogue About the Art of Portraiture' (1906), trans. by Karl Johns, *Journal of Art Historiography*, 5 (2011), 1–18.

Schwartz, Vanessa R., *Spectacular Realities: Early Mass Culture in Fin-de-Siècle Paris* (Berkeley–Los Angeles–London: University of California Press, 1998).

Seemann, Hans Jürgen, *Bild als Widerstreit: Zur Phänomenologie des Bildes im Anschluß an die Untersuchungen E. Husserls. Ein Beitrag zur Phänomenologie der anschaulichen Unmöglichkeit*, Dissertation vorgelegt bei Prof. Dr. Klaus Held (Gesamthochschule Wuppertal: Wuppertal, 2000) <http://elpub.bib.uni-wuppertal.de/servlets/DerivateServlet/Derivate-746/da0001.pdf>.

Semper, Gottfried, *Style in the Technical and Tectonic Arts: or, Practical Aesthetics* (1860–1863), trans. by Harry Francis Mallgrave and Michael Robinson, intro. by Harry Francis Mallgrave (Los Angeles: Getty Research Institute, 2004).

Simmel, Georg, 'The Picture Frame: An Aesthetic Study' (1902), trans. by Mark Ritter, *Theory, Culture & Society*, 11 (1994), 11–17.

Sloterdijk, Peter, 'Architecture as an Art of Immersion' (2006), trans. by Anna-Christina Engels-Schwarzpaul, *Interstices*, 12 (2011), 105–09.

Somaini, Antonio, 'La cornice e il problema dei margini della rappresentazione', *Le parole della filosofia* 3 (2000), 1–12 <http://www.lettere.unimi.it/Spazio_Filosofico/leparole/duemila/ascorn.htm>.

Sparberg Alexiou, Alice, *The Flatiron: The New York Landmark and the Incomparable City That Arose with It* (New York: St. Martin's Griffin, 2010).

Steinmetz, Rudy, 'Les limites de la représentation visuelle. A propos du cadre chez Husserl, Merleau-Ponty et Derrida', *Alter: Revue de phénoménologie*, 15 (2007), 77–101.

– *L'esthétique phénoménologique de Husserl*: *Une approche contrastée* (Paris: Kimé, 2011).

Stella, Frank, Bruce Glaser, and Donald Judd, 'Questions to Stella and Judd' (1966), in *Minimal Art: A Critical Anthology*, ed. by Gregory Battcock, intro. by Anne M. Wagner (Berkeley–Los Angeles–London: University of California Press, 1995), pp. 148–64.

Stidham Rogers, Stephanie, *Inventing the Holy Land: American Protestant Pilgrimage to Palestine, 1865–1941* (Lanham: Lexington Books, 2011).

Stoichita, Victor I., *The Self-Aware Image: An Insight into Early Modern Metapainting* (1993), new, improved, and updated edition, trans. by Anne-Marie Glasheen, intro. by Lorenzo Pericolo (London–Turnhout: Brepols, 2015).

Sweeney, James Johnson, 'An Interview with Mondrian', in *Piet Mondrian: Exhibition Catalogue* (New York: Museum of Modern Art, 1948), pp. 1–16.

Temkin, Anne (ed.), *Barnett Newman* (Philadelphia: Museum of Art, 2002).

Vischer, Friedrich Theodor, *Das Schöne und die Kunst. Zur Einführung in die Aesthetik* (1897), ed. by Robert Vischer (Stuttgart–Berlin: Cotta, 1907), pp. 116–17.

Voltolini, Alberto, 'Visually-Based Knowingly Illusory Presence and Picture Display', *Phenomenology and Mind*, 14 (2018), 158–68.

Walton, Kendall, 'Transparent Pictures: On the Nature of Photographic Realism', *Critical Inquiry*, 11, 2 (1984), 246–77.

Warstat, Willi, 'Der Bilderrahmen. Ein Kapitel angewandter Ästhetik', *Zeitschrift für Psychologie und Physiologie der Sinnesorgane*, 45 (1907), 441–52.

Weibel, Peter, 'The Intelligent Image: Neurocinema or Quantum Cinema?', in *Future Cinema: The Cinematic Imaginary after Film*, ed. by Jeffrey Shaw and Peter Weibel (Cambridge MA–London: The MIT Press, 2003), pp. 594–601.

Wharton, Annabel Jane, *Selling Jerusalem: Relics, Replicas, Theme Parks* (Chicago: University of Chicago Press, 2006).

Wolf, Werner, and Walter Bernhart (eds), *Framing Borders in Literature and Other Media* (Amsterdam–New York: Rodopi, 2006).

Wright, Alison, *Frame Work: Honour and Ornament in Italian Renaissance Art* (New Haven and London: Yale University Press).

Wyss, Beat, *Ein Druckfehler: Panofsky versus Newman – Verpasste Chancen eines Dialogs* (Köln: König, 1993).

– 'La contemporaneità di un medievista: il suggeritore dell'artista', in *Meyer Schapiro e i metodi della storia dell'arte*, ed. by Luca Bortolotti *et al.* (Milan: Mimesis, 2010), pp. 89–103.

Yourcenar, Marguerite, 'How Wang-Fô was Saved' (1936), in *Oriental Tales*, trans. by Alberto Manguel (New York: Farrar, Straus & Giroux, 1985).

Zaloscer, Hilde, 'Versuch einer Phänomenologie des Rahmens', *Zeitschrift für Ästhetik und allgemeine Kunstwissenschaft*, 19 (1974), 189–224.

INDEX

MIMESIS GROUP
www.mimesis-group.com

MIMESIS INTERNATIONAL
www.mimesisinternational.com
info@mimesisinternational.com

MIMESIS EDIZIONI
www.mimesisedizioni.it
mimesis@mimesisedizioni.it

ÉDITIONS MIMÉSIS
www.editionsmimesis.fr
info@editionsmimesis.fr

MIMESIS COMMUNICATION
www.mim-c.net

MIMESIS EU
www.mim-eu.com

Printed by
Digital Team – Fano (PU)
June 2020